FINANCIAL FREEDOM FOR BLACK WOMEN

STOP THE CYCLE OF BEING A BROKE, INSECURE & SCARED GIRL. WALK INTO WEALTH, BUILD YOUR SELF-WORTH, AND DESIGN THE FUTURE YOU WANT

BRIA JOHNSON

CONTENTS

Introduction — v

1. WHY IS IT SO DIFFICULT FOR BLACK WOMEN TO BECOME FINANCIALLY INDEPENDENT? — 1
2. FINANCIAL LITERACY: Take Your First Steps in the Business World and Learn a New Financial Language. — 11
3. ELIMINATE DEBT STRATEGIES — 21
4. SAVING AND BUDGETING — 33
5. INVESTING — 47
6. SIDE HUSTLE OPTIONS — 57
7. EMERGENCY FUND – HOW IT WORKS AND HOW TO SET IT UP — 69
8. RETIREMENT PLAN — 81
9. START YOUR OWN BUSINESS: — 93
10. TEENAGE DIARIES: TIPS ON HOW TO MAKE AN ENTRANCE IN THE BUSINESS WORLD (BEST SAVING STRATEGIES) — 109
11. YOUNG ADULT: THE COLLEGE STUDENT SURVIVAL GUIDE (HOW TO KEEP YOUR FINANCIAL STABILITY THROUGHOUT COLLEGE) — 121

Conclusion — 131

INTRODUCTION

Many black women want to attain financial freedom and independence. In fact, many black women are hungry for financial literacy and want to learn about proper financial management so they can wisely budget, save, invest and pay off their debts.

They have realized that it is possible to build wealth and live very comfortable lives if they change their money habits and start to properly manage their finances. In fact, they are reaching out to find out what they are doing wrong and how to change the bad habits in order to build their wealth as seen in the stories below.

Tracy is a 24-year-old woman and has a 2-year-old baby. Tracy revealed that she does not know how to save and is always broke days after receiving her salary. In as much as she uses her money for basic needs, she does not remain with any cash behind to cover her during emergencies. Tracy will get a higher-paying job in a

INTRODUCTION

few weeks and even though she will be making good money, she knows she needs to start saving for herself and for her son. In addition, even though she believes she can start saving, she lacks the financial discipline to do it. She needs help with saving.

Jackline is a 30-year-old woman who has thousands of dollars in student loans and mortgage. Although she makes her minimum monthly payments every month, she still continues to accrue debt because of her bad spending habits and extravagant lifestyle. She revealed that it is difficult to live within her means and to stick to a budget. She wants to change her financial situation by becoming debt free and going on vacations without feeling guilty.

Maryanne is a stay-at-home mother of three children, who is financially dependent on her husband. She is given some cash daily to spend on household needs but lacks money for her personal needs. Furthermore, she feels humiliated every time she has to ask her husband for money for everything, including her sanitary towels, and he always gets angry whenever she asks for money. She desires to find an online job or part-time job that can enable her to buy her own things and also contribute towards buying things for her home.

All the financial situations that these women are in are completely understandable. Tracy struggles with saving, Jackline struggles with budgeting, paying off her debts and living within her means. On the other hand, Maryanne wants to find some viable side-hustles or online jobs where she can generate income for her needs as well as those of her family.

The good news is, all these women can attain financial literacy and financial freedom by reading this book. It covers topics like;

- Strategies to eliminate outstanding debts
- Budgeting Strategies
- Saving
- Investing
- Side hustle options
- Building an emergency fund
- Opening a retirement plan
- Starting your own business
- Survival guide for students
- How to join the business world as a teenager

Therefore, if you are a black woman and you are in the same financial situation as these women or even worse, don't despair. Just continue reading to find out how you can get yourself out of your tough financial situation to attain financial freedom.

FINANCIAL FREEDOM

The opposite of financial problems, is financial freedom. Financial freedom is the status of having enough wealth or income to pay for your expenses for the rest of your life without having to be employed or financially dependent on other people. Financial freedom may also mean having enough cash, savings and investments to live the lifestyle you and your family wants.

Financial freedom is very broad and may mean different things to different women, as highlighted below. (stories first covered by women magazine)

According to Amrit Kaur, financial independence means being able to live comfortably after paying all her bills, investing and supporting her family without worrying about her next pay check. This means not depending on anyone else's finances, which gives

INTRODUCTION

her a sense of confidence and security. According to Kaur, being financially free gives her a sense of respect and equal standing in her relationship. Moreover, it boosts her morale, enables her and her partner to remain objective and also improves their relationship.

At first, Kylie believed that financial freedom was about helping her family and travelling all over the world. However, overtime, she has grown and believes that financial freedom to her is also about creating a legacy as well as making an impact on other people's lives.

Claire believes that financial freedom is being able to let her children pursue their education and interests without being prevented by the balance in her bank account. She also believes financial freedom is being able to buy whatever she wants without worrying about the price, and being able to work when she wants to without worrying whether her income will be affected or not.

According to Tracy, financial freedom is being able to work whenever and wherever she wants to, doing whatever she wants to do. In addition, it is the ultimate freedom lifestyle.

SUCCESS STORIES OF WOMEN WHO OVERCAME FINANCIAL PROBLEMS AND ATTAINED FINANCIAL FREEDOM

Financial freedom is not attained overnight. In fact, many women have had to dig themselves out of tough financial situations in order to become financially free and independent. Some of these women's stories are highlighted below.

INTRODUCTION

Sarah had $24,000 worth of student loans and consumer debt and felt overwhelmed. Apart from her multiple credit cards which had interest rates that were as high as 29%, she also had over $15,000 in student debt. Sarah used her credit for everything, including car payments and buying a new TV.

Sarah was a stay-at-home mother while her partner at the time was working. She found it difficult to manage the bills and pay her debts because she did not have any income at the time. Sarah revealed that the situation was horrible and she was getting calls from the creditors every single day.

However, Sarah decided to change her financial situation by consulting a finance counsellor who helped her create a realistic budget and a financial outline that would take her from owing the $24,000 debt to being debt-free. She also went through financial literacy training, which helped her prioritize and repay her debts.

During the final six months of payments, Sarah was motivated to see that the debt she had was reducing and she realized she was almost there. When she made her last payment and walked away debt-free, she finally felt free. Now that she does not have any loans, she strictly follows a budget, and has frequent conversations with her new partner about ways they can balance their finances and their lives.

According to Sarah, things have now completely changed because they can look towards the future. In the past, she says there was no future and no savings, but now, they can save for a home and a family vacation. (story originally by moneymentors.ca)

Amina, 30, decided to train in health work after being impressed by a school dental nurse who took care of her oldest daughter when she was little. Amina later met her partner, they started

INTRODUCTION

living together and later had a baby daughter. She then got employed by the local district health board. Unfortunately, in the months that followed, her partner started physically abusing her. She was the only one who was working at the time, and had to hide her injuries whenever she went into the clinic.

Since Amina's wage wasn't enough to cover the groceries, rent and bills and he had a bad credit score, he urged her to take loans from a bank and a finance company. As the interest rate continued to rise, she continued to borrow money from her family and friends, and the debt reached $15,000.

One day, Amina's partner beat her in public so badly that she sustained a concussion and the police finally removed her and her children from the abusive home. She ran to the nearest big city and got treated. She and her children were then given accommodation in a Women's Refuge. She was hiding from her abusive ex and had a protection order against him too.

Moreover, since Amina's name was on the loans and accounts, she was responsible for repaying them and unless she could convince her ex to take responsibility for his share of the loan, she would pay the whole sum.

After six months of living in the Women's Refuge centre, she moved into a rental home for them in the city but her credit record was tarnished. Fortunately, she found a Good Shepard worker who argued her case and the $6,000 debt was written off by the bank.

Amina cried when the debt was halved, and she began to see an end to her tough ordeal. She landed a new job in private practice, and regained some of her self-worth. In less than a year, she had paid off the rest of the debt to her friends and family, and the finance company.

According to Amina, freedom means living within her means and not having to rely on other organizations or people and making her own decisions. (story originally covered by newsroom.co).

BENEFITS OF FINANCIAL FREEDOM

Below are some benefits of attaining financial freedom to motivate you to get your finances on track, like the women above did.

- **It will improve your mental health**

If you are always worried about money, it can negatively affect your emotional wellbeing. However, when you are financially independent and free, you will be able to relax and enjoy your life.

- **You will have more disposable income**

After paying for your needs and recurrent expenses every month, you will have more extra money to spend on whatever you want. This means you will be able to use your money on things that make you happy and on activities that you enjoy, rather than on necessities only.

- **Your lifestyle will improve**

Since you will have more disposable income, you will be able to afford higher-quality services and goods, including nicer clothes, vacations and a nicer home.

INTRODUCTION

- **You will get more free time**

If you aren't worried about money, you will have the time to focus on other things that are important to you, like spending more time with family and friends, taking some time off to relax, or pursue your hobbies and dreams.

- **Your relationships will improve**

When you attain financial freedom, your relationships may also improve. Since you are not worried or stressed about cash, you can focus on your relationships more and make them stronger.

In addition, if you have a spouse, it will improve your relationship because you will feel less overall stress, you will have more quality time together and you may be closer to him or her.

- **You will have access to more opportunities**

When you achieve financial freedom, you will have more opportunities and you will also have the ability to take advantage of those opportunities without worrying about how it can affect your finances.

- **It will boost your confidence**

Financial freedom may make you become more confident. It can help you become more confident in your health, looks, relationships, communication, careers and life choices.

- **You will have less stress**

Financial freedom will lessen your stress because you will not have to worry about having inadequate cash to cater to your expenses. In addition, it will give you more peace of mind and you will feel more at ease.

- **You will have greater financial independence**

If you are financially free, you will have more financial independence. This means you will not depend on other people for financial support. Therefore, you will be in a position to make your own financial decisions and control your future.

By now you may be completely motivated to begin changing your life by changing your money habits. You should know that no matter which financial situation you are in, its never too late to start changing it. All you need to do is learn all about financial literacy and take measures to change how you spend your money.

In addition, you can work with a financial expert who can evaluate your situation and determine the best course of action to take to improve your finances, like setting up a realistic budget that is tailored to your specific sources of income, needs, wants and other expenses.

1

WHY IS IT SO DIFFICULT FOR BLACK WOMEN TO BECOME FINANCIALLY INDEPENDENT?

Many black women want to become financially independent. However, it is difficult for them to do so because of some challenges they go through, but before we discuss these challenges, let's look at what financial independence means.

Financial independence has a couple of different meanings. For instance, you can be financially independent if you are responsible for all of your expenses, without relying on a parent, guardian or other family members to cover your bills using their own money. Financial independence also means the ability to fully meet your basic needs every month by using your income to pay for your daily expenses and to plan for your future.

In addition, financial independence may be the point in life where you do not need to work anymore in order to cover your finances, and you rely on passive income to cater to your needs and wants. Furthermore, financial independence may mean being self-employed, whereby you are running your own business and earning your money without working for someone else or being employed by someone.

There are many black women who have attained financial independence, and other women of colour can do the same. However, many black women face many challenges that hinder them from building wealth and attaining financial independence.

For instance, according to a report on Women in the Workplace by leanin.org, on average, black women in the United States are paid 12% less than white women. In addition, women of colour enrol in college at higher rates than white men, but black women who have a bachelor's degree earn 36% less than white men who also have degrees.

This pay gap impacts many black women, including mothers who are breadwinners in their families, and whose entire household depends on their pay checks. When black mothers are underpaid, they will not have enough money to pay for basic necessities like rent, food and school supplies. In the long run, this will affect the black woman's ability to save, invest, seek higher education and even buy property, which also prevents her from becoming financially independent.

Another reason why women of colour find it difficult to climb the corporate ladder in their careers is because of the racism they experience in their places of work, which can demoralise them or make them be discriminated against when it comes to promotions and rewards, like the stories below, as told by Citywire.

1.

Sometimes when Omotunde Lawal, who is the head of EM corporate debt at Barings, is in a meeting, she notices that the conversa-

tion is usually directed to her male colleagues, even when the women are the ones who hold the highest ranks in the team. Furthermore, when the people in the meeting notice their mistake, they don't turn their attention towards all women in the meeting, but to the women who are white.

Lawal says that as a black woman in a meeting, sometimes people assume that she doesn't know what she is saying, that she isn't going to be articulate and that she is just not competent enough.

Lawal also disclosed that, in the past, she has been left out of jobs because people felt they did not have a lot in common with her, mostly because of her ethnicity, because there was a good ratio of females and males.

Despite climbing through the ranks over the years, Lawal is still unable to bring her 'whole self' to work. In fact, she has had to do code-switching, both as a woman and a black person. For instance, she is trying to tone down her more feminine aspects in order to be taken seriously. In addition, she is also toning down some of her cultural aspects because she does not want to bring her full Nigerian self to work.

Lawal lets people see her western version of herself, in how she behaves, dresses and speaks because she knows that she could very easily be labelled as an angry black woman. So, she is intentional in how she communicates and comes across when interacting with her colleagues.

Concerning the low representation of black women in the finance industry, Lawal believes that there are many qualified black women out there, and that people just need to go beyond their normal pool of talent to find them. In addition, Lawal believes that if people are not open-minded enough to stop their uncon-

scious bias and start supporting black female talent, we won't ever get the representation we need at the top because women won't be in those rooms when the hiring decisions are being made.

2.

Marisa Hall, who is the co-head of the Thinking Ahead Institute, has also experienced racial discrimination in her career. For example, back in 2005 when she was in Leeds for a graduate scheme at an investment firm, she was walking outside her office when one man categorically told her to go back to Africa. Her first thought was, the man was wrong, because she wasn't from Africa, but from Trinidad.

According to Hall, at the time, she felt very alone and isolated because no one looked like her. In addition, she was in the investment industry in the North, and not only was she a woman and black, but also an immigrant.

Hall has also experienced the fear of not being accepted in her workplace which predominantly has white colleagues. For instance, it took her many years to stop straightening her hair because of hair discrimination, and what would be considered professional or not. Hall believes that it can happen, especially in consultancy, where there will be a question of whether they can put you in front of a client or not. Hall has never felt comfortable enough to wear her hair in an afro at work.

WHY IT'S DIFFICULT FOR BLACK WOMEN TO BECOME FINANCIALLY INDEPENDENT

Apart from Racial inequality, workplace discrimination and gender pay gap that hinder women from becoming financially independent, there are other reasons that prevent women of colour from building their wealth like;

Cost of childcare

Women are the primary caregivers and are more likely to take lesser work shifts, quit employment or take time off work among other things. These actions may hinder their financial future by either cancelling or delaying their professional growth.

This in turn may reduce their household income, force them to cut back on spending, and put financial strain on them to the point where they have to borrow money in order to cater to their household needs.

Balancing work and their personal lives

Apart from being employed, many black women also have additional roles as mothers, wives and other responsibilities like taking care of the household. When they try to balance all these roles, they can become emotionally, financially and mentally drained.

For instance, if a woman needs to do household chores like cooking, doing laundry and preparing the children for school, it will affect the type of jobs they can take and how much time they can spend at work.

Difficulty in accessing financial products

Women have a higher risk of being denied financial products such as loans or they can be given smaller loan amounts in financial institutions compared to their male counterparts. Therefore, although women may try to improve their lives by taking advantage of these financial products, they may lack enough resources to create businesses, invest, build wealth or get ahead financially.

Being financially dependent

Some women depend on their spouses financially, or may be relying on alimony if they are divorced. This put them at a disadvantage because if the husband or ex-husband passes away, becomes incompetent or refuses to help financially, the woman and the children may suffer.

Social and cultural norms

It is not easy for people to rise through the ranks in their careers, but it is more difficult for black women to do so. Moreover, women may not be taken seriously if they want leadership roles. In addition, women may be forced to take 'female only' jobs, which hinder black women from job advancement opportunities that can pay them more money and allow them to learn more.

REAL STORIES OF WOMEN WHO BEAT ALL ODDS TO BECOME INDEPENDENT

Although many black women experience challenges in their journey towards becoming financially independent, many do not give up and they end up becoming successful. If the women below beat all odds to attain financial independence, you can do so too. Their stories were first highlighted by Quartz Africa and Caribou Digital.

1.

Afia was working at a debt collection company, but resigned when they were unable to pay her due to the financial hardships brought about by the pandemic. When she stopped getting paid, her husband started providing for everything.

Afia noticed it was not easy for him to be the sole breadwinner because she had to ask him for money to do everything, including going to the salon or buying a toothpaste. When Afia had stayed home for several months without any income, her husband finally allowed her to use the family car to make an income as a taxi driver.

Now, Afia says she will never need to explain to anyone why she wants to buy something or wash her hair at the salon again.

2.

Carol, who is 28 years old, was also fully dependent on her husband before joining Uber and Bolt. Carol's husband did not want her to be a motorbike rider but she explained that the money he was providing daily was not enough to cater for their needs.

Later, Carol and her husband separated, but she continued carrying customers using the motorbike and this is still her only source of income. Carol is able to afford school fees for her children, they eat well, they are clothed and she is able to pay her rent, just from what she earns as an Uber and Bolt driver.

3.

Akoth, 28, is an online writer who gets writing gigs on Upwork, which is a global freelancing platform. Akoth used to be a teacher but the job was underpaying her. According to Akoth, she would always have debts by the time she was receiving her salary and felt like she was wasting herself by working there.

So, she took some money she had saved while working as a teacher and bought a laptop, then underwent training in freelance writ-

ing. Writing has helped Akoth pay her own school fees, her siblings' school fees and some short courses.

REASONS WHY YOU SHOULD BECOME FINANCIALLY INDEPENDENT

Here are some important reasons why every woman should strive to become independent;

You become self-sufficient and self-reliant

Financial independence enables you to pay for most of your basic needs and wants. However, when you depend on someone else, you will have to wait for them to take care of your needs, which can be very frustrating, especially if those people have financial problems or are unreliable. Being self-reliant does not mean that you should never ask for help. It means that you can pay for all your immediate needs and wants using your income.

You are free to make your own choices and decisions

Some women who financially depend on their spouses or partners do not have the authority or power to make major decisions in their marriages or relationships. In fact, you may find yourself in a situation where your partner controls and dictates your life if they are the sole breadwinner in the marriage. This can make it difficult for you to share your opinions or make choices because you don't have your own money or the power to do so.

It prevents abuse

Unfortunately, some women who are in abusive relationships don't want to leave because they financially depend on their partners. If you are financially stable, you can leave an abusive marriage or relationship and support yourself financially. That is why you should prioritise your career and education so that you don't endure abuse because of lack of finances to leave the home permanently.

To keep up with inflation

Inflation has been slowly increasing over the years and now, the cost of owning a good home, enrolling your children in quality schools and maintaining a comfortable standard of living is expensive. Therefore, a household with two incomes is better. If a woman is earning her own money, she can pay some of the household expenses and also contribute to the family's long-term financial objectives.

It increases your sense of self-worth

Although money is not everything, earning an income and spending it however you want will influence how you feel as a person. Women who are financially independent tend to feel more confident about themselves and usually have a higher self-esteem.

2

FINANCIAL LITERACY: TAKE YOUR FIRST STEPS IN THE BUSINESS WORLD AND LEARN A NEW FINANCIAL LANGUAGE.

Financial literacy is the ability to understand and use different financial skills like financial management, investing, saving and budgeting to grow your wealth and achieve financial independence and freedom. Financial literacy builds the foundation for your relationship with your money, and is a skill that can be learnt at any age in life, although the earlier you learn about financial literacy, the better you will utilize your money.

For instance, Emma, who is 27 years old and a high school teacher, understands the importance of teaching her students about financial literacy when they are young. She educates the students on basic financial literacy topics like personal budgeting, education and retirement saving, debt management, investing, insurance and tax planning.

Emma believes that even though these topics may not be very relevant to her students when they are in high school, the financial literacy lessons may be valuable to them throughout the rest of their lives.

For example, if students understand concepts like debt management, interest rates, opportunity costs and budgeting, the knowledge may help them manage their student loans that they may borrow in order to fund their college education and help them to avoid accumulating huge debts, which may ruin their credit scores.

Similarly, topics like retirement planning and income taxes may benefit the students as they grow older, regardless of the careers they end up practicing after high school.

Are you financially literate?

If you know how to create your budget, plan for your retirement, manage your debts and track your personal spending, then you are financially literate. However, if you don't know how to do any of these things, then you can learn to do so in this chapter.

As a woman, lack of financial literacy can affect your life negatively, such as by increasing the risk of accumulating unsustainable debts by spending money poorly. This can result in having poor credit, housing foreclosure, bankruptcy and other negative financial consequences.

The good news is, if you are not financially literate, you can learn some financial skills and implement them to get out of debt, properly manage your money and become financially stable, like the women did in the stories below, as told by Forbes.

1.

When Christina Yumul moved from San Diego to Maui when she was 26 years old, she had accrued about $50,000 in debts from student loans and overspending money on vacations. She made *the decision to change her financial situation by replacing expensive dinners, nightly cocktails and weekend road trips to Las Vegas and Palm springs with hiking, sunbathing at the beach and spending time with her friends in their homes. According to Yumul, these activities provided the same emotional satisfaction without the expensive costs.*

In addition to the lifestyle change, she started paying more than the monthly minimums on her debt and managed to pay off her car within a couple of years. She wanted to buy a new car, but she got engaged to her fiancé. Her fiancé was good at managing his money and did not have any debts. This made Yumul feel embarrassed about the $30,000 loan she was bringing into the marriage and she decided to pay off all her loan before her wedding, which would take place in two years' time.

Yumul signed up for automatic transfers from her pay checks to her loans. Moreover, whenever she went to the grocery store, she only bought what she needed that day and only carried her debit card in her wallet. Her financial discipline enabled her to pay her debts a few months to their wedding.

Although Yumul wanted to feel financially confident in her marriage, being debt-free has meant so much more to her. Now, 33-year-old Yumul who is a public relations executive in Hawaii, has completely changed her spending habits and has her own company. In addition, she and her spouse save money for their goals and are currently budgeting for a trip to New Zealand.

2.

Back in 2005, Paige Hunter and her husband took out a 30-year mortgage, which made her feel like she had a rock tied around her neck. That motivated them to aggressively focus on paying off the loan, which they managed to do within seven years.

The day they completely paid off their debt, Hunter felt relieved and stress-free. Since they both love kayaking, they bought themselves kayaks to celebrate being debt-free. They then set sail on their maiden voyage in the San Marcos River and felt empowered to enjoy their lives to the fullest.

Hunter, who is now 41 years old and works as a business and health coach in San Antonio, says the best part about being financially free, is having the ability to contribute to causes that matter to her, and travelling the world. Since being debt-free, Hunter and her husband have travelled to Asia and visited friends in Japan, went on a boat cruise in Vietnam, explored Angkor Wat in Cambodia and volunteered with a charity in Thailand.

Hunter feels very proud when she remembers they teamed up to completely pay off their mortgage, and they are reaping huge rewards from doing so.

3.

Jessica Jabbar, who is a 27-year-old advertising executive in New York City, felt financially free one day after logging into her bank account and seeing $100,000 of her hard-earned savings. In the six years that Jabbar has worked in New York City, her income has risen from $6 an hour at her first advertising internship to over six figures in her current role.

Jabbar, who has a humble background, who was raised in a small town in South Carolina, believes that living in the big city is an achievement on its own. Jabbar meets her savings goal by setting a very detailed budget and setting limits for all her expenses like entertainment and groceries. In addition, she controls her *spending by following a 24-hour rule when she is shopping, where she waits to see whether she is still thinking about an item the next day, before she buys it. Furthermore, she limits her spending when she wants to go out for dinner by looking for hidden gems where she can spend less.*

Now that she has hit her $100,000 milestone, she plans to start investing so she can earn more profit than the interest rate the cash is getting in a bank account.

Just like these three women, you can also become financially literate and financially free and reap the benefits.

BENEFITS OF FINANCIAL LITERACY

When you become financially literate, you will become empowered to make smarter decisions when it comes to your income.

Financial literacy has the following benefits;

- **It will prepare you for any emergencies**

Financial literacy skills like saving prepares you for any unforeseen emergencies. For example, getting laid off or getting a salary decrease can negatively affect you. However, you can cushion yourself from such problems by putting money into their savings and emergency savings accounts.

- **It will help you reach your goals**

When you fully understand how to budget and save your money, you can create plans that will hold you accountable to your finances and help you achieve financial goals that seem unachievable. For example, although you may not be able to afford something that you would like to do, like travelling abroad, you can create a plan to increase your chances of making it happen.

- **It will help you achieve financial confidence**

When you have knowledge about finances, you can make major life choices confidently knowing that you are less likely to be affected by unforeseen negative outcomes.

- **It will help you avoid making devastating mistakes**

Some innocent financial decisions can have very serious and long-term implications that can cost you money or negatively affect your life plans. However, financial literacy can help you avoid making any mistakes with your personal finance.

STRATEGIES TO GAIN FINANCIAL LITERACY SKILLS

If you want to gain financial literacy skills to improve your personal finances, you need to learn and practice some skills related to managing and paying off loans, budgeting and investing.

Some of the strategies to gain financial literacy skills have been highlighted in this chapter, and discussed in detail in the chapters ahead so you can fully understand them.

They entail;

1. **Create your budget**

Start by writing down the total amount of money that you receive every month against how much you spend on paper, in an excel sheet or with a budgeting app. Ensure that your budget has your;

- Income; pay checks, alimony, child support or profits from investments
- Fixed expenses; rent payment, utilities, loan payments
- Discretionary spending; in this section, you will include your wants, which may include eating out, travelling and shopping.
- Savings.

1. **Pay yourself first**

In this strategy, you will choose a savings goal, like a down payment for a home, decide the amount of money you want to contribute to it every month, and always subtract it first from your income before dividing the remainder of the cash on your other expenses.

1. **Pay bills as soon as you can**

Always pay your bills promptly. You can pay them promptly by automating the payments so they can be deducted every month on time.

1. **Build an emergency fund**

An emergency fund is important because it ensures you are financially covered in case of an emergency like the pandemic or being laid off from work.

1. **Review your credit score**

You can review your credit score once a year and ensure you have a good credit score. A good credit score can help you get low interest rates on loans.

1. **Manage your debt**

Follow your budget to reduce your debt by avoiding overspending and increasing payments. Furthermore, you can reduce your debt by following a debt reduction plan like paying the loan that has the highest interest rate first. If you have a very huge amount of debt, you can contact the lenders and renegotiate the repayment, consolidate funds or enrol in a debt counselling program.

1. **Invest**

You should start investing immediately. In fact, investing when you are young is a great way to see returns on your cash because of compound interest, which will make your investments grow on their own.

You can start investing with little money because there are investments which are available for small amounts of money, like mutual funds, index funds and exchange-traded funds. Moreover, there are investments that have zero commissions and have no investment minimums.

1. **Look for free resources**

You can take advantage of free tools that might be available to you. For example, your credit card issuer, your bank or credit union might track how you spend money on its app or website. You can use these tools know where your money is going and how your credit score is.

Moreover, you can research on whether the company you work for provides an employee financial wellness program or free financial counselling. If it does, then you can speak to a financial professional and gain knowledge on the areas that you need to focus on, like retirement, saving, debt reduction or budgeting.

Additionally, you can seek help from credit counselling agencies, which hire professional counsellors who are certified in debt payoff techniques and budgeting. The counsellors and financial advisors can help you set financial goals, save for college and retirement, and paying down debt.

The Bottom Line

Financial literacy is mostly about preparing a budget, calculating the amount to save, deciding favourable loan limits and distinguishing the different retirement savings plans. These skills are crucial in life because they help you make smarter choices and act more responsibly with your personal finance.

Financial literacy also helps you establish control over your finances and by enabling you to use your money as a tool to freely make choices that help you feel more satisfied in life. Moreover, when you use the correct budgeting strategy, save and track your spending, you can find extra money to enjoy your life, like going on those vacations without feeling guilty.

3

ELIMINATE DEBT STRATEGIES

Being in debt is a very terrible feeling because it looms over you like a dark cloud, preventing you from living your best life and hindering your financial goals, like buying a house, saving for retirement or even going on your dream vacation.

If you have a huge debt totalling thousands of dollars or hundreds of thousands of dollars, you may think it is impossible to pay it all off, especially if you have a low income. Furthermore, you may feel like you are not doing anything with the cash you are putting towards your debt every month, especially if you are making minimum payments and the interest keeps increasing.

The good news is your debt does not need to last forever and you can pay it all off in time if you stick to a plan and follow some financial tips outlined here. If you are tired of owing thousands of dollars in debt, then getting out of debt should be your number one priority for your cash.

If you have doubts about whether you can pay off your huge debts within a short period of time, then you should read the stories below about women who managed to pay off their huge loans which they had accumulated over the years.

Shaarona Harris, who is now 45 years old, works as a full-time multi-media specialist for a think tank in Washington DC. During her free time, she does several side gigs and spends time with her family. When Harris was in her 20s, she accumulated a whopping $80,000 in private and federal student loans after moving from a community college which was state-funded to an American University.

At the time, she was young and thought of the student loans as "free money". She did not have anyone to warn her about how the loans were going to affect her life in the long run. After graduating, her outstanding student loan amount continued to increase. Years later after she got married, her husband pointed out that the minimal payments she was making towards her loans were not lowering the principal of the loans. That's when she discovered she was pouring water into a bucket filled with holes.

Although she and her husband had well-paying jobs, her outstanding loan balance was weighing them down. In order to get herself out of the debt, Harris decided to take a couple of part time jobs like being a certified nursing assistant and caring for hospice patients during the evenings and over the weekends. In addition, she turned her hobby as a master gardener into content for a YouTube channel called The Mocha Foodie Gardener. She also makes extra cash as a brand ambassador for an in-home hydroponic company.

Harris put all her extra income from her side hustles towards paying her debt and managed to slash it by $60,000. She believes she will pay off the remaining $20,000 debt in about two years. (Story by Essence)

Carmen Perez had accumulated a whopping $57,000 of debt which comprised of credit cards, student loans, a car loan and a collections account. Perez realized she needed to act fast when she was sued for her student loans, and feared she would be fired from her job in finance because of the lawsuit.

This was not the first warning she had received as years earlier, Perez had received job offer at a Wall Street investment bank, which was later rescinded after they reviewed her credit report and found out she was defaulting on her student loans. Her position was given to another candidate. Despite the setback, Perez continued living pay check to pay check even though she was earning six figures, and only realized she had serious money problems when she was sued.

Perez, who was raised by a single mother and had two siblings, believed it was possible to overcome her financial obstacles and drew strength from her mother, who believed that when you are at your lowest, you need to find the determination to succeed. Perez then began reading and learning about budgeting, saving and how to pay off debt.

She chose to use the cash envelope method as a budgeting method and the debt snowball method to pay off her debts. Perez paid off all her debts within two years and nine months after starting her plan to become debt free. Now at 35 years old, she cannot believe all the changes she has made in her life. (story by Forbes)

The truth of the matter is, if all these women managed to pay off their outstanding debts, you can do it too. If you are determined to be debt free, you can do it by following the financial tips below;

1. **Stop increasing your debts**

First and foremost, you must stop increasing your existing debt. This means you should;

- Start using cash instead of credit cards for spending.
- Stop taking out more high-interest loans.
- Stop borrowing from friends and family members.
- Stop getting advances from your pay checks.

You may find this step challenging because it will make you look at how you are spending money and how you keep borrowing cash. However, you need to start here, otherwise the process of getting out of debt will become more challenging.

1. **Calculate the total of all your debt balances**

Whether you have a low income or not, you will need to know every single penny of loan that you owe someone else or a financial institution. So, take out all your loan statements and credit card statements and calculate;

- Every single debt that you owe
- The interest rates of each debt
- The minimum monthly payment
- The actual amount of money that you pay every month for each debt

- Your total debt that you owe

If you have defaulted on bills anywhere, you should also add all the fees and penalties that apply to your accounts. Although finding out the outstanding debt you owe might be discouraging, it should motivate you to start paying those debts as soon as possible on your journey to being debt free.

1. **Choose the correct debt repayment strategy for you**

If you have a low income, then you won't be able to put thousands of dollars every month towards offsetting your loans. Therefore, you will need a strategy that will allow you to pay money on your debts on a consistent basis. You can use the snowball or debt avalanche method.

1. **The snowball method**

In this method, you will pay off the smallest debts first and moving on to the next highest amount until you reach the largest debt. This method, which was popularized by Dave Ramsey, who is a personal finance professional, is about slowly gaining momentum. You can pay a lot of money on the smallest debt and make minimum payments to the other loans.

When you finish paying the smallest debt, you roll that payment over to the next loan and repeat the process. You will continue with this method until you pay all of your debts. This method is great because it will give you motivation and a sense of achievement as you wipe out one loan after another.

How to start the snowball method

If you are ready to commit to this snowball method, start with the following steps;

- Write down a list of all of your loans and credit card debts.

- Arrange your list of loans from the smallest outstanding balance to the biggest outstanding balance.

- Start paying off the smallest loan first. As you are paying the smallest loan, also make at least minimum monthly payments on all of your other debts. If you make any extra money, you should use it to pay the smallest debt. For example, if your smallest debt has a minimum monthly payment of $75 and you make an extra cash of $75, you should add the two amounts to make $150 and use it to pay your smallest debt.

- Continue making payments to the smallest loan until it reaches zero. Then move on to the next smallest loan and start using the $150 you were paying on the first loan to the current one, adding it to the monthly minimum payment until it reaches zero as well.

1. The Avalanche Method

The debt avalanche method takes a similar approach to the snowball method, but instead of paying off the loans by the balance, you pay them off using the interest rates instead. Therefore, you will start with the loan that has the highest interest rate and eliminate it, then continue paying until you reach the one with the lowest interest rate.

How to use the Avalanche Strategy

If you want to use the debt avalanche strategy, you should take the following steps;

- Create a list of all of your loans

- Arrange the loans from the one with the highest interest rate to the one with the least interest rate.

- Create a budget to track your salary and how you spend it. If you get extra cash beyond your minimum monthly debt payment, allocate it towards paying off the loan with the highest interest rate on your list.

- After you have paid off your highest interest loan, move to the loan that has the next highest interest rate. Take the amount you were using to pay off the highest interest loan and put it towards eliminating the next highest interest rate.

For example, let us say you have four loans that you want to pay using the avalanche strategy. They will appear in the following manner on your list;

DEBT

BALANCE

INTEREST RATE

Credit Card

$7,000

17.99%

Personal Loan

$6,000

14.99%

Student Loan

$30,000

6.99%

Auto Loan

$15,000

4.99%

In this scenario, you will start by paying off the credit card loan that has the 17.99% APR. Once you have eliminated this loan, you will move on the personal loan that has an APR of 14.99%, and use the cash you were paying on your credit card to pay the personal loan, adding the extra money to the loan's minimum monthly payments. Continue making minimum monthly payments on all your other loans.

If you consistently follow this strategy, you could eliminate all your loans.

1. **Start budgeting your income**

If you are trying to get out of debts, you should take control of your money by starting to budget it. Budgeting can help you pay off your debts faster because it will show you where the extra money is to put towards your loan payment.

In addition, you will know the total amount of money you earn and spend, and what your wants and needs are. From there, you can find out where you are wasting your cash, cut your spending and use the extra money to pay your loans.

However, if you already have a budget, you should find out how to cut your spending.

Action Step: *You can cut spending by cancelling cable and watching television using cheap streaming services like Hulu. You can also switch to a prepaid phone plan. You can also carry the exact cash for buying groceries to prevent buying things impulsively.*

Additionally, you can turn off the lights as you leave a room and unplug appliances that you are not using. If you like having fun with your family members, you should find cheap and affordable ways like going on nature walks.

1. **Start using your money on priorities**

If you want to pay off your loans as soon as possible, you will need to start spending your money on priorities only. First and foremost, you should differentiate between a need and a want. A need is something that you completely need to survive, such as basic things like food, shelter and clothing. On the other hand, a want is something that you don't need in order to survive, like designer clothes, take-out, entertainment or a bigger house.

When you learn the difference between a need and a want, you will be able to cut your expenses and get extra cash that you can put towards your debts. You don't need to live a frugal lifestyle forever, but if you want to pay your loans faster, you will have to make some sacrifices in the beginning.

Action Step; *Evaluate how you have spent your income in the past 30 days and divide every expense between a need and a want. Ask yourself where you could have saved some money and used it to increase the amount of debt payments you make every* *month. This month, try to reduce the money you spend on your wants and put that extra cash towards your loan.*

How to Pay Off Your Debt Faster

Now that you know all the initial steps of how you can pay your loans, you can follow the steps below to pay them faster and get out of debt sooner. These action steps include;

Pay more than the minimum balance

When you start paying more than the minimum balance, you will reduce the overall loan that you have, which means you will pay less interest rate in the long run.

Leave within your means

This means you should not spend more money than what you earn every month if you desire to be debt-free. This does not mean you should live a very frugal lifestyle, but you should be very intentional with your spending.

Get a side hustle

If you have tried to cut your spending but you just cannot find anywhere else to save money, then you may have to find a way to make extra cash. You can earn more money by starting a side hustle or taking a part time job at night or during the weekends.

Use extra money to pay off your loan

If you get extra money from a bonus at your work or a monetary gift, put it towards paying off your loans. Your main focus should be on lowering that overall loan balance.

If you are serious and determined to pay off your debts, then you can do so within a short period if you follow these strategies and stick to them. Consistency is key because it might take some time to fully eliminate all your debts. If you feel demoralized, think about how free you will feel when you have no debts and the kind of life you will start living without a heavy financial load weighing you down. Your lifestyle will also definitely improve when you have no loans to pay.

4

SAVING AND BUDGETING

If you constantly run out of money before your next pay check and you have no idea how you spent it, then you need to start saving and budgeting your salary. A budget is a plan on how you will spend the money you earn and it helps you live within your means, cut costs and grow your wealth. When you create and follow a budget, you will always have enough money to make it through the month, even if you have a low income.

One surprising thing about budgeting and saving your money is, you will feel like you got a salary increase because you will know where your money is going and you can use more of it appropriately. Both budgeting and saving are very important actions that go hand in hand if you want to build wealth.

In fact, budgeting and saving has helped numerous women overcome their financial problems to become financially free and independent.

. . .

Several years ago, Sharita Humphrey, who is now a finance expert and money mentor, was a homeless single mother of two small children and they were living in a motel after they were evicted from their home.

At that time, Humphrey had no savings, and she was living pay check to paycheck. On top of that, she had outstanding credit and medical debts. The debts, coupled with the eviction, made her credit score plummet. Although she and her children were in dire financial crisis, Humphrey knew that she could not give up because her children deserved an address to call their home.

Humphrey decided to turn her situation around by improving her financial literacy. She learned as much as she could about saving, personal finance, debt elimination and credit by going to the public library with her children as much as possible and reading personal finance and development books.

Humphrey then wrote down her goals and started saving a portion of her income every month, created an easy budget to follow, took steps to improve her credit score and eliminated her loans.

Humphrey revealed the entire process of becoming financially stable was not easy for her, and it took a couple of months before she became financially confident. However, the process was worth it because she and her children moved into their new home and she even got a government job.

Humphrey later started her company after leaving her government position. Humphrey advised women who are in a similar situation not to lose hope, as they have the ability to improve their financial situation and create beautiful lives for themselves and their children. In addition, she advised women to shift their mindset and change their money behaviours in order to build a positive relationship with their finances. (Story originally by Yahoo).

When Maya Corbic was 15 years, she and her family migrated from Bosnia with only two suitcases and $50. They did not speak English, her parents were jobless, they were relying on government assistance and living in government housing and shelter.

Corbic was working two jobs by the time she was in high school and supporting herself independently. She was buying items like shampoo and school supplies while also saving for post-secondary education from her income. Unfortunately, she did not manage to save enough and had to take student loans to complete university.

By the time she tied the knot, she and her spouse had accumulated $60,000 worth of debts but she remained positive despite the serious financial problems they had. In order to eliminate the debt, Corbic created a budget and ensured her family was spending less than their incomes. Moreover, although she had a full-time job as an auditor for Deloitte & Touche, she increased her income by becoming a CPA, and used that extra cash to pay their debt.

Corbic and her spouse focused on eliminating their debt and in 8 years, they were not only debt-free, but also mortgage-free. Her advice to women is to build good financial habits. She also advised women who have debts to make regular monthly payments, then increase the amount of payments through budgeting, cutting down on expenses and increasing their income.

Corbic also emphasized the importance of learning personal finance and implementing what you learn. (Story initially covered by Yahoo).

If you are inspired by these women's stories of how they managed to conquer their financial problems, then can start budgeting by implementing the strategy below.

BUDGETING AND SAVING

If you are a beginner when it comes to budgeting, then you can begin with the 50/20/30 budgeting guideline.

1. **The 50/20/30 GUIDELINE**

In this method, you will allocate 50% of your income to needs, 20% towards savings and 30% towards wants. If you follow this simple guideline, you will reduce any debts that you have, increase your savings and have money to spend on leisure and entertainment.

50% Needs

For example, your needs may include;

- Housing (either rent or mortgage)
- Utility Bills
- Groceries
- Minimum loan payments (student loans, credit cards)
- Transportation
- Child care
- Insurance

If your needs pass the 50% mark, you can take some cash from your "wants" portion of the budget.

30% Wants

It is very important to include the "wants" portion to your budget because if you do not have any money for fun or leisure activities, you may be less motivated to stick with your budget. A good budget is one that works well for you and one that you can stick with.

- Travel
- Dining out
- Entertainment
- Gifts

20% Savings

You need to save money to cover unexpected expenses in future, pay off debts or to use on long-term financial goals.

- Retirement savings
- Emergency Fund savings
- Debt repayment on payments that surpass the minimum loan payment amount.

The 50/30/20 guideline will enable you to see how you are spending your money, plan for future costs and emergencies and also allow you to enjoy yourself by doing fun activities.

1. ZERO-BASED BUDGET

The zero-based budget aims at utilizing every single coin you earn. Therefore, in this method, you will allocate all your income to expenses, short and long-term savings and debt repayment. Therefore, your income minus your expenses should equal zero.

The difference between the zero-based budget and living pay check to pay check is, all your financial goals are met. For example, if you earn $3000 every month, everything you buy, save or give, should all add up to $3000. Every dollar has a job, purpose or goal. This helps you avoid spending cash carelessly.

How to make a zero-based budget

1. **Add up your monthly income**

Start by adding up your regular paychecks and extra cash that you will get during the month, like side hustles or child support. The total amount is your total monthly income.

1. **List your expenses**

Now that you know the amount that you bring in every month, start planning for the amount that is going out. List down all your expenses.

Your expenses may include;

- Savings
- Giving, which is usually 10% of your income.
- Needs like food, shelter, utilities and transportation.
- Other essentials like debt, insurance and childcare.
- Month-specific expenses like celebrations, holidays or semi-annual expenses that are due this month.
- Extras like going out to eat at restaurants, entertainment and buying yourself nice things.

Last but not least, you should include a miscellaneous category and leave some cash to cushion you if anything unexpected pops up.

1. **Deduct your expenses from your income**

When you deduct all those expenses from your income, it should amount to zero. If you have some money left, then you can put that towards any financial goal you have, like saving money, paying off debt or investing.

However, if you subtract your expenses from your income and get a negative number, then this means you are spending more that you are earning. The good news is, you can get that number to zero by lowering your spending amounts where possible. Alternatively, you can increase your income by starting a side hustle, taking a part-time job or selling things in order to generate additional income.

1. **Monitor your expenses**

After you have created that budget, you need to track every single transaction to ensure that you are using every single dollar that you earn in the correct budget section to avoid overspending.

If your budget keeps changing from month to month because of those month-specific expenses, then you will need to create a new one every month.

Example of a Zero-based budget

. . .

BRIA JOHNSON

INCOME

Paycheck 1

$3,200

Paycheck 2

$2,200

Side Hustle

$600

Total

$6,000

EXPENSES

Giving

$500

Food

$650

Housing

$1,250

Utilities

$200

Transportation

$300

Debt

$1,000

Insurance

$850

Miscellaneous

$100

Fun Money

$150

Savings

$1,000

Total $6,000

In the above example, you can see that; $6,000 (**INCOME**) - $6,000 (**EXPENSES**) = $0

1. **THE ENVELOPE BUDGET**

This method entails dividing portions of your cash and putting them in different envelopes that have been labelled according to your monthly expenses. This is a great method to use if you have a habit of overspending when you use credit cards.

When you use cash instead of credit cards, you will have the hands-on experience that will enable you to strictly follow your budget. This is because, the cash in every envelope needs to last for the entire month because once you use it, you cannot replenish it until next month.

When implementing this method, you can pay for your fixed costs online or via check. Fixed costs are those expenses that do not change every month, like rent, utilities, mortgage, loan payments and insurance. Then, you can use the envelope system for costs that fluctuate every month, like transportation, groceries and utility bills that fluctuate.

You should calculate the amount of money that you usually spend on these expenses, withdraw the cash, then put the allotted cash amount into the different labelled envelopes and open them as you spend. If you notice that some envelopes become empty before the month ends, you can make some adjustments for the next month, like cutting down some costs.

This method is effective if your goal is to stop overspending. It can also motivate you to keep going if you see some remaining cash at the end of the month.

1. **VALUES-BASED BUDGET**

Values-based budgeting is all about making an intentional effort to use any money that is remaining after purchases, on causes that are in line with your beliefs and values. For example, you may look at your spending records and realize that you always use the remaining money after paying expenses, on dining out.

But, if you also like donating to organizations and charities, you can divide the extra money and give some to charities and spend the rest on your own wellness and entertainment.

For example, you can allocate your extra money in the following ways;

- Use 40% of the remaining cash on your favourite dining spots or try foods in new restaurants that have recently opened up.

- Allocate 30% of your extra cash to social programs, local businesses and organizations whose work is in line with your values and beliefs.

- Use the last 30% of the cash to do well-being workshops or self-improvement courses.

When you use this value-based approach, you will feel more aligned with your purpose in life. It can also help you build connections with your local community, and it will also give you a voice.

1. **PAY YOURSELF FIRST BUDGET**

This method helps you to focus on prioritizing your savings. In this method, you will first note your monthly net income. Then, rather than listing all your monthly expenses or dividing your income into percentages or categories, you will write down your monthly savings goals.

Then, you will subtract your savings total from your monthly net income and use the remainder of the money toward paying other expenses and bills.

An example of this budget is;

- Monthly net income; $4,800

- Monthly savings goals: Emergency fund ($500), Retirement fund ($600), Vacation fund ($450), House renovation ($200) = $1,750.

- Money to spend: $4,800 (net income) - $1,750 (savings) = $3,050.

- Use the remaining $3,050 to pay for all the remaining monthly expenses.

This method is suitable for you if you want to protect their futures without being constrained to the traditional budgeting methods. In addition, you will always you're your savings goals.

So, now that you have these budgeting and saving tips on your fingertips, you need to choose one budgeting method and stick to it in order to notice positive changes and growth in your finances. Remember to diligently follow your budget and adjust it accordingly every month in order to achieve your financial goals.

5

INVESTING

Investing is a perfect way to grow your money. It is the act of buying financial assets like bonds and stocks, with the expectation that those assets will increase in value overtime and earn you profits in the long run. There are many different types of investments that are accessible to every person, regardless of your age, career or income and they have been covered in this chapter.

Black women can increase their wealth by purchasing assets at very low prices and selling them at higher prices in future. Investing is a great way to enable your money to outpace inflation and increase in value over a long period, like it did for Tiffany James.

Tiffany James had just graduated from college, had a student loan debt and was struggling to survive financially when one of her coworkers advised her to use one pay check to purchase stock in

Tesla back in 2019, when their shares were $60 to $70 each. That was the investment Tiffany had ever made.

James managed to turn her initial investment of $10,000 to over $2 million by investing in more long-term growth companies, semi-conductor chip stocks and S&P SPDR exchange-traded funds among other investments.

Furthermore, at 25 years old, James founded a community called Modern Blk Girl, whose aim is to teach black women the importance of wealth creation and investing. Now, the community has over 225,000 people, who are mostly women. She believes that when a woman is educated, the whole village will be educated, and if a mother starts investing, she will teach her kids how to do so too.

James, daughter of Haitian and Jamaican immigrants, admitted that investing is not something that was often talked about by people of colour. However, James, who is 27 years old now, believes that black women should not be afraid to invest because it is a necessity if we want to build wealth. Moreover, she believes that investing will open doors to greater financial freedom for women and give them the independence to do what they want. (Story initially posted on CNBC).

Another inspiring story is that of Barbara Corcoran, who used a $1000 loan to start a lucrative real estate firm in New York City. Corcoran was the second oldest of 10 children, and grew up in Edgewater, NJ. Her father was a printing press foreman and her mother a housewife.

Corcoran would score Ds in school and was labelled a 'dumb kid' by her classmates in school. Before even graduating from St.

Thomas Aquinas College, she had done over 20 jobs, from being an orphanage housemother to selling hotdogs. After college, she met her boyfriend Ray Simone, a builder, while she was waitressing. He loaned her $1000 and they started a business in 1973, called Corcoran-Simone, and he got 51% ownership of the company and she started working as a rental agent in Manhattan.

The company grew exponentially over the years and they had hired 14 agents and had an annual revenue of around $560,000 when her husband Simone, told her he wanted a divorce so he could marry her secretary. In 1978 as they were dividing their company, Simone told Corcoran that she could never succeed without him. Corcoran said those words branded her soul and she founded the Corcoran Group to prove that she was capable of succeeding on her own.

At the time, there wasn't any real estate firms that were owned by women. In an effort to stand out, Corcoran started wearing bright colours and short skirts to stand out from the crowd and although she did not feel welcomed, she was noticed. Within the first year of starting the Corcoran Group, she had 7 agents and revenues totalling $350,000.

By 1993, her company was selling real estate online, 2 years before their competitors. In 1988, she was married to Bill Higgins, who was operating his parents' real estate firm. She later became a mother at 46 years old, after being on in vitro fertilization treatments for 8 years. It was what led her to sell her company.

In 2001, Corcoran realized she had achieved her dream of becoming the top broker in New York. At the time, she had 850 salespeople and about $97 million in revenues. She sold her company for $66 million to Henry Silverman, the chairman of NRT.

If these women used the money they had to invest in businesses and stocks that generated profit for them over the years, you can do it too. If you want to invest, you should start with what you have and do what you can. After all, we all start from somewhere.

Here is what you need to know before you begin investing your cash to reap profits;

1. **Begin investing as soon as possible**

You should start investing immediately. In fact, investing when you are young is a great way to see returns on your cash because of compound interest, which will make your investments grow on their own.

You can start investing with little money because there are investments which are available for small amounts of money, like mutual funds, index funds and exchange-traded funds. Moreover, there are investments that have zero commissions and have no investment minimums.

If you think your contribution may not be enough, you should select an amount that is manageable to you. For instance, you can contribute as much as $5000 or as little as $50 a month to your investments, as long as you are being consistent, and you will reap the profits.

For example, if you contribute $200 every month to your investment for 10 years and get about a 6% annual return, at the end of the 10 years, you will have accumulated $33,300. Out of the $33,300, $24,200 will be the $200 monthly contributions you were making, and $9,100 will be the interest that you have earned on your investment.

Therefore, if you want to see your money growing over the years, you should invest immediately, even if you have to start with a small amount.

1. **Decide on the amount you are willing to invest**

You should choose the amount you want to invest in depending on your investment goal, financial situation and when you want to reach your goals.

1. **Patience is key**

It is very important to remain patient if you are a new investor because long-term investments usually yield more profits because your investments will need more time in order to grow. Your investments will also need time to adjust to the changing economic situation of the market.

For instance, stocks can plunge and there can be an economic recession that lasts for months or years. If you sell your stocks when there is a recession in the market, you may lose a big part of your investment. Therefore, if you want to reap fruits, you should invest your money and remain patient without acting out of fear when the market dips.

1. **Risk and Investment**

In order to become a great investor, you should know your risk tolerance. This will help you decide on the best investment options. For instance, financial products like bonds are less risky than stocks. This is because when you purchase stock, there is no guarantee that you will get profit. For instance, if a company does not perform well or if it loses investors, the company's stocks can drop and you can lose money.

On the other hand, government bonds are relatively safe because they are usually insured. However, the only downside is the returns from government bonds are lower than profits from stocks.

Therefore, if you want to gain profits from your cash, you should find the right balance between risk and reward, and put your money in both high-risk and low-risk investments.

INVESTMENT OPTIONS

1. GOVERNMENT BONDS

A government bond is a loan that you give to a government body, such as the municipal government or the federal government, and you start receiving interest on the loan over a specific period, which could be anywhere from one to thirty years. Government bonds are a form of fixed-income security, because you will be receiving the consistent stream of payments over the long duration.

In addition, government bonds are risk-free, because they are backed by the credit of the government of the United States of America. However, one disadvantage of putting your money in government bonds is, you will not get a high amount of return compared to other types of investment options.

Best for: This is suitable for women who do not want to take high-risk investments because bonds continue to go up even when stocks plummet, which prevents nervous investors from panicking. Furthermore, since bonds have a fixed-income and less risks, it is popular among women who are nearing retirement or have already retired since these individuals may not have enough time to endure unexpected and sudden severe market declines.

Where to buy it: You can purchase individual bonds from the U.S government, from the underwriting investment bank or from a broker.

1. **CORPORATE BONDS**

A corporate bond is a loan that you give to a company. Since these loans are not backed by the government, they are riskier compared to government bonds.

Best for: women who want to take more risk by investing in corporate bonds with a fixed-income security and higher profit returns than government bonds. When it comes to corporate bonds, the higher the chances of the company going out of business, the higher the profits you will yield. On the other hand, corporate bonds that are issued by stable companies usually have lower profits.

Where to buy it: You can purchase individual bonds or corporate bond funds through an investment broker.

1. **MUTUAL FUNDS**

A mutual fund collects cash from investors in order to purchase bonds, stocks and other assets. This enables investors to diversify by spreading their cash across many different investments to minimize the damage of any single investment's losses.

Best for: Women who are saving for long-term goals like retirement.

Furthermore, some mutual funds limit their investments to companies based on a specific criterion like tech companies, so this will enable you to focus on certain investing niches.

Where to buy it; You can access mutual funds through discount brokerage firms or directly through the companies managing them. Mutual funds usually require a minimum initial investment of around $500.

1. EXCHANGE-TRADED FUNDS (ETFs)

ETFs collect money from investors and use it to purchase a collection of securities, to provide a single diversified investment.

Best for: ETFs are suitable for people who have a long-time horizon. In addition, they are perfect for people who do not have enough cash to pay the minimum investment requirements for a mutual fund.

Where to buy it; You can buy ETFs through brokerages.

1. INDIVIDUAL STOCKS

A stock refers to a share of ownership in a corporation or company. Stocks provide the highest potential profit on your investment but it also exposes your cash to the highest risk.

Best for: women who have invested in other options and are willing to take on additional risk by purchasing stocks too.

Where to buy it; You can purchase stocks through an online broker.

1. REAL ESTATE

The traditional process of investing in real estate entails buying a piece of property and selling it later to gain profit. It also entails owning property and collecting rent from tenants as fixed income.

Best for; women who have already invested in other options, and are willing to take on more risks for more profit. Since real estate investments are not liquid, you should not put money into real estate if you need to access the cash quickly.

1. DIVIDEND STOCKS

Dividends are cash payments that companies pay to shareholders on a regular basis to reward them for owning stock. Dividends are associated with profitable companies that are stable.

Best for: Dividend stocks are best for first-time investors to retirees.

Where to purchase it: you can easily buy dividend stocks through an online broker.

1. CERTIFICATES OF DEPOSIT (CDs)

These accounts have a higher fixed interest rate compared to most savings accounts. CDs are usually short-term or medium-term investments. If you have deposited your money in the account, you cannot access it until the maturity date, which can be between 6 months to 5 years.

1. **I-BONDS**

I-bonds are government debt issued by the United States Treasury. The interest rate of I-bonds is adjusted after every 6 months to keep pace with inflation. Even though I-bonds have advantages, the one disadvantage is, you have to leave the money untouched for 5 years so you can keep all the interest that has accumulated. Furthermore, you are only allowed to buy $10,000 worth once a year, although you can add $5,000 of your tax refund towards I-bonds.

If you want to become a successful investor, you should first consider the risks and rewards and your financial goals and purpose. Then, you can use all the information highlighted above to make informed decisions when selecting the investment option that is suitable for you.

6

SIDE HUSTLE OPTIONS

Money is something that everyone needs more of, whether you need to make ends meet, save more, invest or pay for debt. If you already have a job to cater to your basic needs but you need more money to supplement your income, you can start a side hustle.

There are many remote side hustles which give you the opportunity to work from home, so if you already have a 9-5 job, you can do the side hustle during your off days, after work or even during holidays and earn extra money to make your life more comfortable.

Moreover, there are some side hustles that allow you to earn passive income, therefore, once you start them, all you have to do is relax and let the money come in. Side hustles can be a game changer that can make a big impact in your purse, and if you do it right, you can successfully turn your part-time job into one of your main sources of income.

If you still doubt that you can start a side hustle whilst working your 9-5 job, then you should read the story below, which was initially posted on cnbc.com.

Tina Meeks first started posting about motherhood on Instagram in 2015 because she felt very lonely as a new mom. Meeks, who was 27 years old at the time, and her husband James, who is an entrepreneur in the tech space, had just moved from Phoenix to Dallas.

Meeks, who was working a full-time job as an insurance adjuster and earning a salary of $55,000, had no one to talk to about the challenges of parenting a 5-year old and a new-born baby and she felt very isolated. She felt like no one seemed to understand what she was experiencing, not even her spouse.

Therefore, she turned to the internet to share her challenges with women going through a similar situation, who could understand her and encourage her. Therefore, she started sharing the ups and downs of juggling motherhood and her full-time career.

She named her Instagram, "Her Life Sparkles", after her childhood nickname, sparkles. She started giving recommendations on family, home décor, fashion, parenting, relationships and haircare. In addition, she posted pictures of her kids in Halloween costumes and food.

Within the first year, Meeks had made a whopping $1,000 from collaborating with brands. To her, it was a side hustle that was supplementing her 9-5 job of being an insurance adjuster.

In 2018, Meeks became pregnant with her third child and although the pregnancy was unplanned, it turned out to be a stroke of good luck for her brand, which grew exponentially. She gained more followers, from 2,000 to 10,000. Furthermore, the *floodgates opened a few months later, when brands started reaching out to her, with the aim of partnering with her. Diaper, clothing and soap brands among others wanted her to market their products because she had created a very shoppable life on social media. In fact, thousands of mothers were always eagerly waiting for the next product she would recommend or any photo that would help them get a glimpse into the relatable mommy life they were also going through.*

Meeks decided to invest in her business when she realized the potential growth of her brand. She studied photography and bought a professional camera, which paid off in the long run. For instance, when the pandemic broke out, the companies she had partnered with, including Fab Kids and Children's Place, could not shoot or create their own ads because of the strict safety restrictions that were put in place to combat the spread of the virus.

That's when she decided to put her photography skills to good use. She offered her services and became a one-woman digital marketing studio. For starters, she turned her kids into little models since her three children fit into every age bracket; a school-aged child, a toddler and an infant. She then started shooting different types of content for brands in the comfort of her own home.

In 2020, Meeks earned a whopping $300,000 just from collaborating with brands and advising aspiring mom influencers on how they can grow their businesses. In the end, she resigned from her full-time job and turned her side job into her main source of income. Meeks, who is now 35 years old, has managed to build a very lucrative brand and she currently has an Instagram following of 148,000 people.

Meeks story shows that we can manage to balance a 9-5 job and a side hustle and, if done correctly, we can even turn our side hustles into our main sources of income.

Therefore, if you are struggling to make it to the end of the month because you don't earn much from your 9-5 job and you are looking for ways to gain more money on the side, then you can try some of the side hustle options below.

ONLINE SIDE HUSTLES

1. Blogging

Blogging is a great job to do on the side because you can write about what you are passionate about, at your own pace, anywhere you want. There are many ways to earn money while writing. For instance, you can advertise products and services of brands on your blog, do affiliate marketing for other people's products, sell your own products online and more.

If you want to start blogging, you need to be patient because it will take time to build an audience in order to earn a decent amount of money. However, once you build a large following, you can make over $15,000 per month. You can start your site on Bluehost, HostGator or Hostinger, which have cheap monthly costs.

1. Sell crafts on Etsy

If you are creative, you can open an online shop on Etsy and sell your crafts to people who are looking for unique products. For example, you can sell knit hats, home décor products themed around the holidays, custom embroidered handkerchiefs or cards and invitations.

1. **Online freelancing**

There are a lot of clients that are looking for freelance writers, editors, graphic designers and transcriptionists among other professionals on platforms like Upwork, Freelancer and Fivver. Therefore, you can earn money by registering in any of these online platforms, applying for jobs from the clients and getting hired to work for them.

If you are just beginning to use a freelance writing platform, you can accept low-paying jobs in the beginning in order to build your reputation on the platform by getting good reviews. This will help you attract high-paying clients and high-paying.

1. **eBook publishing**

If you have a story to tell or important skills to share, you can write an eBook and sell it on Barnes and Noble or Amazon.

1. **Sell Stock Photos**

If you are a great photographer who is passionate about taking photos, you can sell your photos on online sites like iStockPhotos, Alamy, Shutterstock, Getty Images and Stocksy. You can earn money through commissions every time someone downloads your image from a stock photo site.

Therefore, the money you earn will depend on how popular your pictures are and how often they get downloaded. Moreover, commissions vary from site to site. For example, Shutterstock pays around $0.25 to $80 per download.

1. **Create a course online**

If you can teach something to people, you can create an online course on Udemy.com, Teachable, Thinkific or LearnDash. You can create a course for almost any topic on earth and you can charge the price that you feel is appropriate for your course.

The good thing about creating an online course is, you can do so with little to no investment, and it will provide you with a monthly return for months or years to come.

1. **Sell used goods on eBay**

If you have old items such as outdated light fixture or furniture that you have replaced, you can sell them on eBay first rather than throwing them away. There may be someone in the market who may be looking for the exact items that you do not need.

1. **Become a Virtual Assistant**

You may enjoy using social media, writing or even blogging but you don't want to start your own site. If you are in this situation, you can search for virtual assistant jobs where you can assist other people to run their social media accounts and sites. In addition to working for an individual, there are many big companies that are looking for virtual assistants to outsource their administrative work to.

You will enjoy helping the companies with administrative tasks and keeping their accounts and blogs active. In addition, you can start earning more money as your skillset also improves.

1. **Teach English online**

If you are a teacher or you have a degree from a College or University in the United States, then you can teach English to children and adults in other countries virtually. For example, you teach using VIPKid, which is a platform that bridges the gap between native English speakers who have degrees with children in countries like India or China.

You can create a "class" time and the children will signup for your class virtually. You will earn cash when you teach. The interesting thing about teaching online is, you can make $14 to $22 per hour online, just from the comfort of your own home.

Another platform that you can explore is Preply, which connects English teachers with students from over 180 countries around the globe. In addition, you can set your own hourly rate and create your own teaching schedule. Furthermore, you can teach other subjects like French, Math and Art.

1. **Monetize your Instagram Account**

You can start creating engaging content on a specific niche that you are passionate about and use strategic hashtags to build a social media following. Once you have gotten over 10,000 followers, you can begin earning money by monetizing your posts and partnering with advertisers.

OFFLINE SIDEHUSTLES

1. **Become a Lyft or an Uber Driver**

Ride-sharing is a great side hustle because you can do it in your own time, when its convenient for you. All you need is a car and determination to earn extra cash. You can begin by signing up with uber and after you have been cleared as a drive-partner, you can start driving people to their destinations.

If you want to maximize your chances of earning more money, you can sign up to both Lyft and Uber and use both apps simultaneously.

1. **Baby Sitting**

Babysitting is a good job for teenagers, college students and young adults, who can earn cash by looking after neighbours' and relatives' children during their free time. In addition, there are online services that can connect babysitters with parents, which makes it easier to get bookings. One example of an online platform that connects sitters with parents is Care.com.

1. **Assist people with their resumes**

If you are a hiring manager or you work in HR, you can put your skills to use during your free time by helping other people with their cover letters and resumes at a fee. You can even do this job online through email or skype for many clients.

1. **Do Makeup for special events**

If you are good at doing makeup, you can earn extra money by doing people's makeup before big events or photoshoots. You can market yourself online or partner with a photography company where you can easily get access to clients who need makeup services before doing their photoshoots.

1. **Become a Model**

This is a great side gig for people who are passionate about modelling and the fashion industry. You can find a balance between going to school or work and doing modelling gigs on the weekends and in the evenings.

When you are starting out, you may not get a steady stream of income but if you succeed in a few gigs, you can start earning good money from it. You can start by checking online classified ads for modelling cast calls.

1. **Become a Movie or TV Extra**

There are many studios that are always looking for extras and depending on where you live, you can become an extra on a movie or TV show. In addition, you can be paid hundreds of dollars just for walking or standing in the back of a movie set.

You can search for adverts looking for movie extras on platforms like Backstage Extras Casting.

1. **Bake**

Everyone loves eating fresh-baked cakes and other delicious treats, but not everyone can make them in their kitchens. Therefore, if you have the passion and talent of making delicious cakes, then you can start a baking business and sell your treats.

1. **Gardening and Painting Services**

If you reside in a place where people need gardening services, you can knock on their doors and offer your gardening services. Additionally, you can look at online classified ads for gardeners who need assistance with their existing projects on sites like Craigslist.

Painting service is also a good side gig for college students. If you are free during the summer or weekends, you can either paint houses or partner with painting companies and get work. Although painting is not an easy job, you can get paid very well in the right estates and neighbourhoods.

1. **Teach music lessons**

If you know how to strum the guitar or play the piano, you can join a local music group or sell your services to schools that need music tutors. You can teach students how to use musical instruments and even help them create musical pieces to perform during inter-school competitions and during special school events and occasions.

1. **Refurbish and resell used furniture**

You can purchase beautiful pieces in thrift stores and improve their appearance by adding a coat of paint, adding some new drawer pulls or even changing the fabric of the furniture. You can then resell the furniture and earn a good profit.

1. **Sell handmade candles and soap**

You can purchase a soap-making kit at your local supermarket or craft store and create sweet-scented soap in your home and sell them online. Additionally, you can create sweet-smelling handmade candles and sell them.

After you have built a big client base, you can start custom-making candles or soaps for your clients per their request. If your products are being purchased in large quantities, you can turn this passion into a full-time job.

1. **Start a cleaning business**

You can charge people an hourly rate or project-based rate for cleaning their homes during your free time. This is a good gig because it does not need a lot of money to start and you can keep improving and growing the business every single month.

1. **Become a wedding and events planner**

You can learn the right skills and collect the right contacts before starting a wedding planning business on the side. If you are consistent, it can become a lucrative business.

1. **Teach Yoga**

If you are already a certified yoga instructor, you can earn cash on the side by working as a part-time yoga instructor during the weekends.

1. **Become a Tour Guide**

If you live in an area with a lot of tourist attraction sites that attract millions of visitors every year, then you can start a local tour guide business as your part-time job and earn extra cash.

You can do some of these part-time gigs for women even if you are already working full-time and see which one goes well with your schedule and lifestyle. You can utilize extra cash to improve your lifestyle, pay off your debts, go on vacations, save or invest.

7

EMERGENCY FUND - HOW IT WORKS AND HOW TO SET IT UP

An emergency fund is money that you set aside so you can use it when you are in financial distress. The main aim of building an emergency fund is to improve your financial security by creating a pool of funds that you can use to meet unexpected and sudden expenses, like unemployment (for example, when millions of workers lost their sources of income when the pandemic broke out worldwide), sickness and major house or car repairs.

When you have an emergency fund, you will not need to borrow high-interest debt options like unsecured loans or shylocks when you are experiencing a financial crisis.

Some women may argue that it is difficult to create an emergency fund when they are already living from pay check to pay check. In fact, there are women who have nothing in their savings account to cushion them because of many reasons like the increasing cost of living, redundancies caused by the pandemic and rising interest rates.

BRIA JOHNSON

Below are real stories of women who don't have any money in their savings accounts.

Matilda is an audio editor who is 26 years old and earns a salary of £22,000. According to Matilda, the reason for having £0 in her savings account, is because she never seems to get enough money to pay all her bills. In fact, she never remains with any extra cash after paying her bills.

Unfortunately, her savings account balance is always £0 because she was never taught anything about money as a child and never developed the mindset to put any money aside for emergencies. Now that she is older, the habit has continued because she has bills to pay and is dealing with the high cost of living. Matilda also revealed that she doesn't have a good relationship with money.

Sara is 23 years old and works in the social media department at a start-up company. She earns a salary of £27,000. Sara has no cash in her savings account because she pays for almost everything for her disabled parents. Growing up, her family accrued a lot of debt so half of her salary is used to pay for bills, food and the debts. Sara reveals that although she is good at budgeting, she finds it difficult to save if she does not earn enough money to begin with.

In addition, Sara finds it difficult to save because she uses any disposable income to treat herself. Sara prefers to live comfortably instead of saving for any rough patches in future. She does not believe in saving small amounts of money, and would rather spend it immediately.

. . .

Katherine, who is 34 years old and works as a curator at a museum, makes a salary of £33,000. She admits that her zero balance at the bank is due to paying her credit cards, which exist because she has had to use them to live. As soon as she finishes paying her debts, she doesn't remain with enough money to survive till the end of the month, and uses her credit cards again.

In addition, Katherine admits she has never had a good relationship with money, and cannot control her impulsive buying. Moreover, she always ends up paying back huge interests on her debts. Unfortunately, she cannot see herself buying a house or getting out of the bad financial cycle because her credit rating is also bad.

Some of the women above have a bad relationship with money and have failed to save anything for future emergencies due to their low incomes and huge debts. So, the question is; is it possible to build an emergency fund if you are living from pay check to pay check?

CAN I BUILD AN EMERGENCY FUND IF I AM LIVING FROM PAY CHECK TO PAY CHECK?

It is possible for you to create that pool of funds for any unexpected emergencies if you are living from one pay check to the next. However, it won't be easy and instead of worrying about your total savings amount, you should decide on the amount of take-home pay that you can live without.

For instance, you can decide to set aside 1% or 2% of your salary for the emergency fund. The important thing is to save the amount you have decided to set aside every payday and not touch it. The money will accumulate over time.

If you are still undecided about whether you really need an emergency fund, you should read the experiences of these women whose emergency savings saved them in the long run.

A WOMAN WHOSE EMERGENCY SAVINGS SAVED HER

Maryanne was unfortunate enough to experience a storm in her residential area, which flooded her basement. The water damage is so extensive that she cannot save the flooring and will have to replace the entire flooring.

In addition, the edges of the floorboards in the basement have wilted because of the water that has accumulated underneath it. Moreover, water was seeping in from behind the dry wall in her basement bathroom. The water has completely damaged her home and unfortunately, none of the losses will be covered by insurance.

However, Maryanne and her family are very lucky because they have about 6 months' worth of living expenses in an emergency fund. The money in that savings account is enough to cover the $15,000 they will need to waterproof the basement. Furthermore, it can cover the money needed to replace the flooring.

Maryanne admits that when she remembered she had an emergency fund, a sense of calm came over her and she knew they were going to be okay. According to Maryanne, the emergency fund will prevent them from having more sleepless nights, and their financial preparedness will enable them to cover the unexpected and sudden losses caused by the storm.

HOW TO SET UP YOUR EMERGENCY FUND

1. **Set a target**

You should calculate the total amount of living expenses that you and your family will need for a certain period of time, like 3 or 6 months. The total amount should cater to all your needs and wants for that duration.

1. **Set a proportion to save from your salary**

You should then set a proportion of your income to go towards the emergency fund account. You can do this by putting money in your emergency fund every time you receive your salary. When you do this regularly, you will slowly develop the habit of saving regularly, which will make the whole process less daunting.

1. **Automate your savings**

Making your saving automatic is one of the best ways to save consistently and see your emergency fund building over time. One way to do this is by setting up recurring transfers through your credit union or bank, so your money is automatically moved from your checking account into your savings account.

You will have to decide how much money should be transferred to the emergency account and how often it will be done, but after you have set it up, you will be contributing consistently to your savings account.

However, you should be mindful of your balances to avoid incurring overdraft fees when you don't have enough cash in your checking account when the automatic transaction is being done.

If you want to be mindful, you should set up calendar reminders or automatic notifications to check your balance.

Who is it helpful for: It is beneficial for women who have consistent income.

1. **Save your tax refund**

You can save your tax refund by having it directly deposited into your emergency fund.

1. **Utilize one-time opportunities to save**

During certain times of the year, you may get a lot of money, like during holidays and birthdays when you may receive cash gifts. You can also get additional cash if you have a side hustle that is successful. Although you may be tempted to spend this cash, you can save all or some of it. This will help you to quickly save a lot of money in your saving account.

Who is it helpful for: This tactic is beneficial for people who have irregular incomes.

1. **Evaluate and adjust your contributions**

You should evaluate your emergency fund account after a few days to see how much you have saved and make the necessary changes, like adding more money if you have recently withdrawn some cash from it. If you have saved enough to cover 3 or 6 months' worth of expenses, you can use any additional income to invest.

WHERE SHOULD YOU KEEP THE MONEY?

The place where you will put your emergency fund will depend on your situation. However, you should ensure that your fund is safe, accessible and somewhere where you will not be tempted to withdraw and spend it on non-emergencies.

Some options of places where you can save your emergency fund include;

A bank or credit union – Banks and credit unions are considered some of the safest places to put your money. Therefore, if you have a bank or credit union account, then you can use it to save and maintain the emergency funds.

Prepaid card – This refers to a card which has money. The card is not connected to a credit union or a bank and you can only spend the money which has been put on the card.

Cash – Another option is to keep cash at hand for emergencies, either in your house or with a trusted family member or even a friend. However, this is not the safest way of keeping your emergency fund because money can be stolen, it can get lost or can even be destroyed.

WHEN YOU SHOULD USE YOUR EMERGENCY FUND

Sometimes, you may be tempted to use these funds to pay off debts, go on an extravagant holiday or make a deposit on a new home. This is why it is very important for you to create a list of expenses that are acceptable for using this emergency fund.

The list of expenses should be true emergencies like covering your living expenses during periods of unemployment, medical emergencies, repairing your home after natural calamities, unexpected veterinary bills, unforeseen vehicle repairs or any other emergency.

The main aim of an emergency fund is not only to cushion you during financial emergencies, but also to prevent you from accruing any debts in times of need. For instance, if you lose your job, your emergency fund will allow you to recover quickly without needing to borrow any loans from lending institutions.

However, you should ensure that you have safely stored your money in your account and that you can easily access it when you desperately need it. In addition, when you put it in a bank, it can continue growing on its own by accruing interest.

REASONS WHY YOU NEED AN EMERGENCY FUND

1. **To avoid accruing more debts**

An emergency fund can help you to stop adding to your debts whenever you encounter any financial challenges. It can help you to cover things you have not budgeted for, such as medical expenses and vehicle repairs. You can use the emergency funds to handle financially stressful emergencies, which will in turn help you to stay focused on your path towards becoming debt free.

1. **If are new at budgeting**

When you begin budgeting, you can mistakenly leave out some very important expenses that you need to plan for. In such instances, the fund can help you to cover those expenses during the first year, and then you can add them into your budget in future.

1. **If you only have one stream of income**

If you only have one job, then you should have a substantial emergency fund. The fund can help you and your family to get out of emergencies like illnesses that prevent the breadwinner from working or unexpected job losses. When you have money that can cover your expenses for at least 6 months, then it can cushion you and your family if the unexpected happens.

1. **If you are self-employed**

If you are self-employed, if you are on a job contract or if you are an independent contractor, then you need to put sufficient funds in place. In addition, if you see that the contract is coming to an end, you should work hard and save up more in your emergency fund.

1. **If you own your own home**

When you are a homeowner, you need to pay for any necessary maintenance or repairs. Even if you have set up funds for repairs and remodelling, there are unexpected costs that may occur, like plumbing issues or flooding problems caused by natural calamities. Your emergency fund can make it less stressful to own a home.

1. **If you have medical issues**

Having a serious or chronic medical condition can be financially, emotionally and physically draining. In addition, it can make you finish all your hospital insurance every year.

Furthermore, routine medical tests and check-ups can add up quickly. Moreover, it can cause you to use up all your sick leave days and force you to take days off without any pay. A good emergency fund can help you cover your medical costs and get through these challenging times.

1. **If you live far away from your loved ons**

If you live abroad, then it can be very costly to travel back home during emergencies and the costs are usually higher during holidays. Having a sufficient emergency fund can help you to cater for last-minute tickets to travel back home for medical emergencies, funerals or even celebrations.

1. **If you are saving for something**

If you are saving towards something and an emergency occurs, your emergency funds will prevent you from using your other savings. This will prevent you from being pushed behind on your path towards saving towards your other goal.

WAYS TO QUICKLY BUILD YOUR EMERGENCY FUND

1. **Multiply your streams of income**

If you want to build your emergency fund quickly, you can diversify your income streams. You can do this by starting a side hustle and putting this money in your emergency savings account. In addition, if you get any unexpected bonuses or returns from investments, then you can put that additional cash into your emergency funds.

1. **Eliminate debt**

You should work hard to completely eliminate your debts so the extra cash being used to pay off those debts can be channelled towards your emergency funds.

1. **Adopt great financial habits**

In order to successfully set up and maintain your savings, you will need to adopt good financial habits like budgeting, cutting down on unnecessary expenses, avoiding impulse buying, investing, living within your means and avoiding overspending. When you do these things, you will have some extra cash to put towards your fund.

1. **Track and monitor your expenses**

Many women are guilty of not knowing where their money has gone to, days after receiving their pay checks. If you are one of those women, then you need to start evaluating and tracking your expenses. You can do this by creating a list of expenses and eliminating the extra expenses that you do not need.

In conclusion, there are many benefits you can get by setting up an emergency fund, like living a more fulfilling life, keeping yourself out of debt, accomplishing your financial goals and building financial discipline through saving.

8

RETIREMENT PLAN

Retirement planning is what you do to prepare yourself for life after you stop working when you attain the retirement age. It involves setting aside enough money to cover all your expenses when you stop working during retirement. Although everyone should strive to put aside enough funds to support them when they retire, some women fail to do so because of many different reasons and end up working in old age in order to cover their living expenses.

Below are some experiences of women who failed to set up retirement funds and how it affected their lives.

Maria Rios, who is 75 years old, has been working as a food prep worker with Contractor HMS Host at Phoenix airport for 17 years, and

earns $14.50 an hour. Her husband has retired and gets only $400 per month in social security benefits. Although Rios would *also like to retire like her husband, she does not have that option, even as she is fighting ovarian cancer.*

When the pandemic struck, Rios was among thousands of workers who were fired in the food service industry, and was only rehired a couple of months ago. While she and her spouse were receiving unemployment assistance, they had to depend on food banks to get enough food to eat. Furthermore, since she had lost her health insurance when she was laid off, she was forced to skip cancer treatments until she got Medicare, and still had to pay out of pocket for treatments which amounted to hundreds of dollars.

According to Rios, people should be able to have pensions and retire with dignity so they won't be forced to be in a position like hers, 75 years old and still working to make ends meet. (story originally covered by theguardian.com)

A couple, Glenn and Mary, had bad financial habits and would always spend their money as soon as it reached their bank accounts. They had never attained financial discipline, and they did not learn how to live within their means or budget properly. At the age of 59 and 47, they had only managed to save $5000 in a 401(k), they did not have any pensions, they had only $300 in their bank account and they had debts of $10,000 on their vehicles and $250,000 on their mortgage.

Although they later learned how to create a budget and Mary got a higher-paying job, their bad spending habits put them farther away from retirement. (story originally covered by machenwealth.com)

. . .

Lynn's parents did not save much for retirement. When her father passed away, her mother did not have any money to her name and she had very little money coming in from social security benefits. Because of this, Lynn had to completely change her lifestyle to have her mother live with them so she could support her.

This changed Lynn and her family's financial lives and she had to adjust their retirement plan as well. Not saving for retirement can cause an unnecessary burden on your children's lives and can also lead to resentment. Although Lynn is able to support her mother and her lifestyle, not everyone else is that lucky.

FINANCIALLY DISCIPLINED WOMEN WHO HAVE STARTED SAVING EARLY

There are women who have decided to start preparing for retirement early in order to be financially ready when they attain the retirement age. These women include;

Jamila is 29 years old and has already saved $41,500 in a retirement account. She started saving for retirement when she got her first job at 22 years old. She was earning a salary of $30,000 annually and contributed 4% of that amount.

Jamila doesn't remember when she found out about saving for retirement, but when she was growing up, she always thought about how much she wanted to retire early because she did not want to work when she was old. Although Jamila's mother never saved money when she was working, she had a pension. Jamila was determined not to be like her mother when it came to savings and handling money.

Jamila got another job in 2018 and started saving 6% of her salary for retirement. She has been increasing 2% every year, and is currently at 14%. She makes almost $80,000. Jamila admits she is proud that she is saving. According to Jamila, many of her friends have not yet started saving for retirement and others are saving very little. She believes in saving more now so she can enjoy the benefits later.

Deborah is 40 years old and has saved a whopping $89,000 in a 403(b) and a 401(a). She started saving for retirement at the age of 24 with her first job. She was making a salary of $28,000 and was contributing 5% of her salary, while the university where she worked contributed 10%.

At the age of 28, she changed jobs and started making $38,000. She continued contributing 5% of her salary while the university chipped in 5%. She did that job for 10 years and managed to save a lot of money. Deborah revealed she feels comforted knowing she has a significant amount of money to cushion her in future.

If you also want to be like these women who have started saving money for retirement but you don't know where to begin, then you are in the right place. Let's begin with the most important thing, the total amount of money you want to save for retirement.

HOW MUCH MONEY DO YOU NEED TO SAVE FOR RETIREMENT?

Remember that you need to start preparing for retirement before you retire. In fact, the sooner you begin saving for retirement, the better. The amount of money that you specifically need to retire comfortably is very personalized. However, the total sum of money you will need to retire will depend on the person you are asking.

For instance;

- Some people say you need about $1 million to retire comfortably.

- Other professionals recommend the 80% rule. According to this rule, you need enough money to survive on 80% of your income when you retire. For instance, if you were making $100,000 every year when you were working, when you retire, you need savings that could generate $80,000 every year for about 20 years, or a total of $1.6 million.

- In addition, other people say that retirees are not saving enough money to meet those high benchmarks, and that they should adjust their lifestyles to live on what they have managed to save.

Although the total amount of money that you want to save in your retirement account is important, you also need factor in all your expenses.

EXPENSES THAT YOU SHOULD FACTOR INTO YOUR CALCULATIONS

- Housing costs, which also include your rent or mortgage, as well as water and heating maintenance.
- Health care costs
- Your day-to-day living expenses like transportation, food and clothing.
- Entertainment, including going to plays, movies and restaurants
- Travelling, including hotels, flights or gas if you are driving.
- Possible life insurance

STEPS TO RETIREMENT PLANNING

1. **Create a plan**

You should create a plan that clearly highlights when you want to start saving for retirement, when you plan to retire and the total amount of money that you would like to save for your retirement.

1. **Decide the monthly contribution to your retirement account**

You should decide what portion of your monthly income will go to your retirement account. In addition, you can set up automatic deductions to keep you on track and prevent you from stopping or forgetting to deposit the money on your own.

1. **Choose the right retirement plan**

There are many retirement plan options that you can choose from and they have all been covered under this chapter.

1. **Check your investments**

You should always evaluate your investments from time to time and make the necessary periodic adjustments, whenever there are any changes to your lifestyle or if you have entered a different stage in your life.

RETIREMENT PLAN OPTIONS

There are many different types of retirement accounts and they all have different rules and regulations that need to be followed. They include;

1. **Employer-Sponsored Plans**

If you are a young adult, then you should utilise employer-sponsored programs like the 401(k) and the 403(b) plans. The 401(k) plan is a retirement account that is provided by major corporations while the 403(b) is used by employees of public schools and charities.

One major advantage of these plans, is your employer can match your contribution up to a certain amount. For example, if you contribute 6% of your yearly income to your retirement account, then your employer can match that amount by depositing an equivalent amount into your retirement account also. Therefore, you will get a 6% bonus that will grow over the years.

In tax year 2023, people below 50 years old can deposit up to $22,500 of their yearly income to a 403(b) or a 401(k), some of which can be matched by their employer. Moreover, people who are above 50 years old can deposit an extra $7,500 every year as a catch-up contribution.

Other advantages of having a 401(k) plan include; earning a higher interest rate compared to a savings account, and having pre-tax contributions. This means the money in your retirement account will not be subjected to tax deductions until you withdraw them during retirement. Therefore, you will enjoy an income tax break.

1. **Traditional Individual Retirement Account (IRA)**

This retirement account allows you to contribute pre-tax dollars. This means that the retirement contribution is deducted from your income before taxes are deducted from your salary. However, when you start withdrawing the money during retirement, tax will be deducted from it.

In addition, the IRS limits the amount of money that you can contribute to a traditional IRA every year. The limit for the year 2023 is $6,500. However, people who are 50 years old and above can contribute an additional $1,000, to attain a total of $7,500 in 2023.

If you select the traditional IRA as your retirement plan, then you must take your total funds at the age of 72. However, you can also take them as early as 59 and a half years old. If you make withdrawals before attaining the age of 59 and a half years, then you will be subjected to a 10% penalty.

1. **Roth Individual Retirement Account (IRA)**

This retirement account is funded using post-tax dollars. This means tax is deducted from your income before you contribute to your retirement account, which reduces a bigger income tax bite when you start withdrawing the money during retirement.

When you start a Roth IRA early, it can truly benefit you in the long run, even if you start with a small contribution amount. This is because, if your money stays in a retirement account for a longer period, it will accrue more tax-free interest.

Both the traditional and Roth IRA have a contribution limit, which is $6,500 annually or $7,500 if you are more than 50 years old.

1. **SIMPLE Individual Retirement Account (IRA)**

This retirement plan option is offered to employees of small businesses, instead of the 401(k), because it is cheaper to maintain. The SIMPLE IRA allows employees to automatically save their money through payroll deductions. In addition, they can utilize the option of an employer match. The contribution limit for this retirement plan is $15,500 in 2023, which is an increase from $14,000 in 2022.

Employees who are 50 years old and above are allowed a catch-up contribution of $3,500, which increases the contribution limit for them to $19,000.

STAGES OF RETIREMENT PLANNING

Even though you can start saving for retirement at whatever age you may currently be, the sooner you begin, the better.

1. **EARLY ADULTHOOD (AGES 21-35)**

If you are embarking on adult life, you may not have a lot of extra money to invest in retirement, but you have the time to let the investments mature overtime. Your investments will increase based on the principle of compounding.

1. **MIDLIFE (AGES 36-50)**

If you are middle-aged, then you may be dealing with a lot of bills like mortgage, student loans, credit card debt or insurance premiums, along with daily living expenses. However, you should continue to save at this stage because of the combination of earning more money and still having enough time to invest in retirement.

If you are in this stage of retirement, then you should continue utilising 401(k) matching programs that your employer is offering. In addition, you should try to make full contributions to a

Roth IRA or a 401(k) or both at the same time. However, if you are not eligible for a Roth IRA, then you should consider a traditional IRA.

In addition, you should not neglect disability insurance and life insurance. This can enable your loved ones to survive financially without withdrawing from retirement savings should anything happen to you.

1. **LATER MIDLIFE (AGES 50-65)**

Even though time is running out for people who are saving for retirement in this age bracket, there are still a few advantages of saving. For instance, you may probably have a higher wage or you may have already paid off expenses like mortgage, credit card debt and student loans. This will leave you with disposable income which you can deposit to your retirement account.

In addition, it is never too late to start saving for retirement. For example, one benefit of contributing to retirement while you're in this age group is having access to catch-up contributions. For instance, if you are 50 years old and above, you can deposit an additional $1,000 annually to your Roth or traditional IRA, and an additional $7,500 annually to your 401(k) in 2023.

Additionally, if you have used all tax-incentivized retirement savings options, then you can explore other forms of investment to increase the money in your retirement savings. For example, you can use blue-chip stocks, certain real estate investments and certificates of deposit to add to your retirement funds.

Moreover, you can evaluate what your social security benefits will be and at what age you can start receiving them. The eligible age for early benefits is 62. However, if you want to get full benefits, then you need to attain the retirement age of 66 years.

This is also the age-bracket where you should start looking for long-term care insurance. Long-term care insurance will enable you to cover the expenses of home care or nursing home if you will need it in old age. If you don't factor in any health-related expenses, especially the sudden and unexpected ones, they can drastically reduce your savings.

9

START YOUR OWN BUSINESS:

Starting a business is a very interesting, rewarding and fun experience. Unfortunately, many women desire to start a business but they don't know where to begin. The good news is, you can stop guessing and improve your chances of successfully starting your business by following the steps and tips outlined in this chapter. However, before you begin, you should get in the right mindset.

There's no overnight success

Many people often hear about overnight business successes because they are great headlines in news. However, building a successful business is not that simple because the public rarely sees the years that entrepreneurs spend dreaming, building and positioning their brand before launching it to the public. For this reason, you should focus on your business journey without measuring your success against someone else's.

You should be consistent

Many business owners tend to rely on their motivation to get work done in the beginning, but they get frustrated when the motivation dissipates. This is why you should follow routines and create habits that can help you to get work done when the motivation goes away.

Take the next step

Even though some black women dive in headfirst and adjust their businesses as they go along, there are others who never take the first step and remain stuck in analysis paralysis. The best way to get out of this cycle is to write down all the steps it takes to achieve your business goals. Some steps may be done in minutes while others may take years. However, you should always take one step after another without getting stuck.

HOW TO START YOUR BUSINESS IN STEPS

1. **Create a business idea**

When formulating your business idea, you should ensure that it is something you love, it is profitable, and you are good at it. For example, if you love music and want to be a musician, you should also ensure you are a great singer and songwriter, and that you can get paid to put out music and perform on stage.

In addition, your business idea can be a new product or concept that improves the lives of people. However, you can also take a product that exists in the market and improve upon it.

What type of business should you start?

- Before you select the type of business to start, you should consider;

- The type of funding you have
- The time you will invest in your business
- Your location; if you want to work in an office, from home or in a workshop.
- Your passions and interests
- Whether you can sell a product or information, like a course
- The kind of support that you need to start your business
- Whether you will be partnering with someone else
- Whether the franchise model makes more sense to you

Popular business ideas

If you are not sure about which business you want to begin, then you can consider starting any of the following businesses;

- A cleaning business
- A clothing business
- A blog
- A franchise
- An online store
- A consulting business
- A photography business
- A landscaping business
- A vending machine business
- A franchise
- Bookkeeping business
- A drop shipping business
- A restaurant

1. Conduct research on your competitors and market

You should not spend more time on your product than getting to know your competitors, because both are equally important. You should figure out what makes your business stand out from the competitors by conducting a market analysis. If you discover that your service or product is saturated in your area, then you should find a different approach.

For example, if you want to offer housecleaning services and many of your competitors are offering general cleaning services in your area, then you can choose to specialize in homes that have pets or on garage clean-ups.

The types of research to conduct on your competitors and market

Primary research

The first stage of studying the competition is the primary stage, which is all about getting data and information directly from potential customers. You can obtain this data through questionnaires, interviews and surveys to discover what the potential customers want.

You should not survey your loved ones unless they are your target audience. This is because your loved ones can say they will buy something and end up not buying because the product isn't something they would actually buy or use.

Secondary research

This entails using existing sources of information like a census data to gather information about your potential customers. You can study, compile and analyse past data to get the answers you need, it may not be as detailed as the information you will get from primary research.

Carry out a SWOT analysis

SWOT in full means; strengths, weaknesses, opportunities and threats. When you conduct a SWOT analysis, you will be able to get the facts about how your business idea may perform if it is launched to the public, and it can enable you to make decisions about the direction of your business idea. Using this analysis can also help you identify some weaknesses that you had not considered or opportunities that can enable you to improve on your competitor's product.

1. Create your business plan

A business plan outlines all the aspects of your business and the steps you will take to establish your new business. Moreover, it will help financial lending institutions, potential investors and the company management to understand your business idea. If you plan on financing your business yourself, then a business plan will help you to flesh out your idea and identify potential problems.

A great business plan should include the sections below;

- **Executive summary**

The executive summary talks about the new business idea, the goals your company plans to achieve and the methods you will implement to achieve those goals.

- **Company description**

The company description will cover the problems that your services or products will solve and why your business idea is better than the rest.

- **Organization and Structure**

Here, you will write about the type of business structure you want to start, the person that will hire the management team and the strategies of managing risk.

- **Market analysis**

The market analysis section is all about analysing how well your business is positioned against its competitors. In this section, you should include your target market, the market size, segmentation analysis, growth rate, a competitive environment assessment and the trends.

- **Mission and goals**

In this section, you will write a short mission statement, what the business wants to accomplish and the steps it will take to get there. Your business goals should be SMART (specific, measurable, action-orientated, realistic and time-bound).

- **Products or services**

This section will highlight the type of products you will offer to the consumers, how your products compare to the products of existing competitors and how much they cost. In addition, you will also include details like who will be responsible for creating the products, how you will source the raw materials and how much the production cost is.

- **Marketing plan**

The marketing plan entails the characteristics of your services or products, it analyses competitors and also summarizes the SWOT analysis. In addition, it highlights how you will promote your business, the amount of money you will spend on marketing and the duration of the marketing campaign.

- **Background summary**

This may be the most consuming section to write. When writing the background summary, you should compile and summarize any articles, data and research studies on the trends that can either negatively or positively affect your business or the industry you are in.

- **Financial plan**

The financial plan is a very crucial section of the business plan because if you don't have money, then your business will not move forward. When creating the financial plan, you should include the proposed budget and projected financial statements like the income statement, a statement of cash flows and a balance sheet.

If you want outside funding, this is also the section where you will include your funding request.

1. **Select your business structure**

When selecting your business structure, you should factor in how each structure will affect the amount of taxes you will pay, the daily operations of the business and whether your personal assets will be at risk.

- **Sole Proprietorship**

In a sole proprietorship, the company and its owner are considered the same, for tax purposes. In sole proprietorship, the owner is liable for the business. Therefore, if the business fails, then the owner is financially and personally responsible for all the debts the business has accrued.

It is very easy to form sole proprietorship business, and you won't need to file a lot of paperwork with your state. In addition, you are the one who will completely control your business.

- **LLC**

A limited liability company can be owned by one or multiple people. LLCs provide the owners with protection and they are among the easiest businesses to set up.

- **Limited Liability Partnership (LLP)**

An LLP is mostly used by licenced business professionals like lawyers and accountants. In addition, such arrangements need a partnership agreement. In a limited liability partnership, the partners have limited liability for the loans and activities of the company. Additionally, it is easy to form LLPs and there is no limit to the number of partners in an LLP.

- **Corporation**

Corporations provide liability protection to the owners. In addition, the lifespan of the corporation is not limited. In addition, it can have an unlimited number of shareholders. Moreover, a corporation can be taxed as an S-corporation or a C-corporation.

1. **Register and license your business**

After you have chosen the business structure, you now need to address some legal issues. They include;

- **Choosing your business name**

You should choose a business name that is catchy and memorable. You should also choose the same domain name and establish your online presence.

- **Register the business**

You will create an LLC, a corporation or any other business structure through filing forms with your state's business agency. You must also pay a filing fee. The state will then give you a certificate which you will use to apply for a tax identification number (TIN), business bank accounts and licenses.

Next, you will apply for an employer identification number by submitting your application to the IRS. All businesses, apart from sole proprietorships, need to have an EIN.

1. **Open your business bank account**

You should separate your business and personal finances. When opening a business bank account, you will have to provide the name of the business and your business tax identification number.

You can use the business bank account for all business transactions like invoicing customers, paying suppliers and receiving a business loan or line of credit from lending institutions.

1. **Fund your business**

There are two categories of funding your business, internal and external funding. Internal funding includes credit cards, personal savings and funds from your friends and family.

On the other hand, external funding includes small business grants, venture capital, small business loans, angel investors and crowdfunding.

1. **Apply for business insurance**

You must have insurance for your business, whether you don't have any employees or you're operating a home-based business. You should work with an insurance agent to know which insurance coverages are suitable for your business.

The basic types of business insurance coverage include; property insurance, liability insurance, product liability insurance, business interruption insurance, workers' compensation insurance and employee practices liability insurance.

1. **Buy helpful business tools**

Business tools will help you to operate your business better. Moreover, they can save time and resources, and automate tasks. Some of the important business tools that you can purchase include;

- Accounting software to track your business expenses and income.
- A customer relationship management software to automate customer service.
- Point of sale (POS) to process your customer payments.

- Project management software to plan, complete and track business projects.
- In addition, you can get email hosting to create an email address that is very professional using your own domain name.

10. Promote your business

You should market your business by creating a business website, optimizing your site for SEO, creating relevant content, getting listed on directories, developing a social media strategy and scaling your business.

TIPS TO SUCCESSFULLY START A YOUTUBE BUSINESS

YouTube is the most popular video-only social media platforms in the world and has as many as 2 billion viewers per month. Therefore, if you have been dreaming of starting your own YouTube channel and earning money from it, then you should start as soon as possible.

However, it is not easy to just create your YouTube channel and become an overnight success and sensation. It may take a lot of time and effort before you can start earning money from YouTube but if you use the right tactics, you will be on the path to success.

How to start a YouTube business;

1. **Create your channel**

Go to YouTube, click on "sign-up" and create your YouTube business account. You will need to fill in the information by selecting a profile name, a cover picture and fill in the "About" section.

The "About" section is where you will describe what your channel is all about. You can tell your brand story here. You can also add your contact and other important business information in this section.

1. **Conduct research**

Before creating content, you should do thorough research to determine who your target audience is. You need to know the demographic of your target audience, like their ages, gender, geographical location, preferences, wants and needs before you begin creating content for them.

1. **Plan and upload your content**

Content creators take a lot of time to plan their content. It Is not just as simple as uploading random content online. You should choose the type of videos that you want to make for your target audience. The type of content that you will create will depend on your type of business and the demographics of your audience.

For example, product-based businesses may find that their audiences love tutorial videos, while service companies may discover that their audiences love hearing about their brand stories.

In addition, you should plan ahead and have a content calendar that will enable you to post consistently without running out of ideas.

1. **Optimise your YouTube video titles and descriptions**

YouTube is the biggest video search engine globally, and you should use YouTube SEO for your YouTube channel. For instance, you should optimise your channel using relevant keywords so it can rank higher in search results when people search for those keywords.

In addition, since your channel only has video content, you should incorporate those keywords in your titles and descriptions. Moreover, you should keep your titles relevant, short and catchy.

1. **Market and promote your YouTube channel**

You may be creating the best content in your niche on YouTube, but people won't even know about it if you don't promote it. Therefore, you can improve your channel's discoverability by promoting your individual videos on other platforms too.

For instance, you can direct viewers from other social media platforms to your YouTube channel by sharing teaser videos about upcoming videos on the other platforms like Facebook, WhatsApp groups, twitter and Instagram.

If you have a business site, you can also place your YouTube links on your website. Therefore, if you want to get more views and engagement on your YouTube videos, then you need to cross-promote your content on other platforms.

1. **Evaluate your progress and improve**

You should evaluate and monitor YouTube's built-in analytics tool. The tool will help you to know how your videos are performing. In addition, the tool also gives you the demographics about your audience and the keywords that are making your videos rank higher. You can use all this information to fine-tune your SEO strategy.

In conclusion, you can start a business if you are determined and willing to stick to your business until you start to make profit and get returns. Every black woman can start and run a successful business if they follow the correct guidelines and steps on starting a business and remain consistent.

10

TEENAGE DIARIES: TIPS ON HOW TO MAKE AN ENTRANCE IN THE BUSINESS WORLD (BEST SAVING STRATEGIES)

If you want to start saving money as a teen, then you are in the right place. You may want to save your money to buy the latest iPhone, your very first car or even save for college. The good news is, saving cash is simple. It just involves spending less than you earn every month and putting the extra money somewhere safe.

If you still think it's difficult to save as a teenager, then you should read stories of these people who started saving as children and how that behaviour is benefitting them in adulthood.

Aaron Shapiro, who is the CEO and founder of Carver Edison in New York, started saving a few cents in a jar every single day when he was a child, to buy the things that he wanted. Overtime, he began saving a few dollars every day instead of cents as he started earning more money and getting bigger goals.

When he became a teenager, he started automatically depositing his money into a savings account, which turned into advanced savings and investment accounts when he became an adult. According to the CEO, when you learn how to set goals and save for the things you want as a child, it easily becomes a habit in adulthood. (Story originally by Forbes).

Darrel and his younger brother Lucas, started a lawn mowing service when they were in middle school. They worked together on their business until Darrel finished high school. Darrel learned very valuable financial lessons from operating their business when he was growing up. Such lessons include; the benefits of keeping great accounting records, great work ethic and compounding interest.

Now, Darrel is 29 years old and has a bachelor's degree without any student debts. In addition, he owns a home, has a very healthy savings account balance and a retirement account with over $40,000.

Jay Ferrans, who is the president of JM Financial and Accounting Services in Southfield, Michigan, started selling fruits and vegetables from a truck when he was only 10 years old. He would work after school, on Saturdays and during the summer holiday. He was paid $5 for a full day's work and he was also given tips.

Instead of spending his earnings on candy, he saved his money in the bank. After a couple of years, he purchased a snowblower and started snowploughing for neighbours. He started earning more money from this work, and got into the habit of saving his income. This saving habit enabled him to get so much more financial freedom to purchase large items as he grew up. According to Ferrans, the financial choices he made while growing up determined his financial wellbeing in his adulthood.

Monica's family had a bad relationship with money. In fact, they lived from pay check to pay check or they would spend more than they earned. This caused them to experience multiple bankruptcies. Monica saw how the financial problems put so much stress on her family, (which has now separated), and vowed she would never end up in the same situation ever again.

Monica got a job and started saving the income to go to university. She managed to pay for her college fees, and completed her studies. After college, she became an avid saver, even though she was already living way below her means. For instance, she was saving 50% of her income from a high-paying tech job. She became excited at her progress and invested money into her knowledge, and eventually became a millionaire in her 20s.

Monica learned a lot of hard financial lessons and grew from them. Monica's experience is a great example that people from different financial backgrounds can become successful, if they are determined to change their situation and gain financial literacy by investing in it.

A few years ago, Sarah began talking to her 12-year-old daughter about saving and investing. Sarah then opened a savings account for her daughter. When the savings accumulated, they invested in it. Her daughter researched companies she was passionate about and invested in those. Her daughter is very proud of her financial accomplishments and always talks about it to her friends and family members.

If you are a teenager and you are inspired by these real-life stories and you want to start saving your own money too, then you can do so by following the tips below. In addition, if you are a teen's parent and you want to help your teen learn about saving, then you can share these tips below with your teen sons and daughters.

WHEN SHOULD TEENS START SAVING CASH?

A lot of teenagers start thinking about saving their money in banks after getting their first jobs. However, teenagers can start saving money even if they do not have any jobs. The best times for teens to begin putting money away include;

- When they land their first jobs
- If they want to buy their own car
- Before going to college if they want to pay for their rooms and other college expenses.
- If they get extra money that they do not need immediately.

HOW A TEENAGER CAN SAVE MONEY

There is no one in the world that is born knowing how to manage their finances. To gain financial literacy, you need to learn, practice, try and even fail a few times in order to become perfect at managing your finances.

Before you begin to save money, you need to earn money, because you cannot save what you do not have. So, below are ways that you can earn money as a teenager.

1. HOW TO EARN MONEY AS A TEEN

Some of the most common ways that teenagers get money include;

Earning an allowance by doing chores

Talk to your family members about chores which they find cumbersome to do and ask them whether they would be willing to give you an allowance after you complete the task.

If they agree, you should take advantage of that opportunity by saving as much as you can towards a specific goal that you have. Keep in mind that the more chores you will complete, the more money you will get and the more savings you will accrue.

Getting a part-time job

You can look for a part-time job at a coffee shop, a local restaurant, a store or a camp. If you're not old enough to land a job in these places, then you can ask your parents to look for people in the neighbourhood who are looking for a tutor, babysitter, lawnmower or a car-washer.

You can also look for paid internships which can allow you to get the experience needed to pursue a career in the same field in future, while being paid money for it.

If you get a part-time job working after school, during weekends or during the summer, you can save money fast since you will be earning a substantial income. In addition, it will enable you to have experience in the workforce.

However, if you are planning to get a part-time job, you should make sure that you can balance your studies and the job. Although it is really nice to earn money, you should not sacrifice your studies for it.

Getting a job during the summer holiday is ideal for most teens because they usually have enough time to make a substantial amount of money while still being able to enjoy their vacation.

Starting a business

If you love baking cupcakes, making smoothies, washing cars, livestreaming to all your fans or playing video games, then you can turn these hobbies into a business. However, you will need to factor in things like; whether you will need to use money to buy software or equipment, the price you will charge for your product or service, and whether you will get paid through cash, cheques or online payment methods.

You will also need to open a bank account for your business. Starting a small business as a teen may seem overwhelming, but if you succeed, it will change how you live the rest of your life.

Holding a garage sale

Holding a garage sale can be a very fun, profitable and rewarding activity that can help you get a lot of cash at once. If you want to hold a successful garage sale, you should begin by organizing all your products into different categories so the buyers can know where to look when browsing through your things.

The next step is to advertise your sales by putting up advertising posters on your neighbourhood or on social media sites like Facebook. The final step is to keep an open mind and be willing to negotiate with potential buyers.

Sell second-hand items

You can sell new or second-hand items that you have not used for a long time on apps like Ebay, Depop and Poshmark to make extra cash. Take Emma's story for example.

Emma Johnson has been selling clothes on Poshmark since she was 13 years old. She has managed to grow her savings and earn money while studying. Emma managed to run her hustle by setting aside time between classes and during the summer holidays to list clothes that were trending.

According to Emma, the clothes would be bought quickly, at good prices. Not only has she developed entrepreneurial skills from selling clothes on the app, but it has also enabled her to gain the experience needed to pursue a career in fashion.

Saving your money gifts

When your loved ones give you money as a gift, don't spend it immediately. Instead, save it in your savings account. This will help you to remain focused on your saving goals instead of using the cash immediately.

1. HOW TO DEVELOP GOOD MONEY HABITS AS A TEEN

As a teen, you will need to practice a few good habits that will help you to save and spend your money wisely. You will also need to adopt a good money mindset that will help you to prioritize your savings goals instead of spending all your cash on short-term impulses.

These good money habits include;

Open a savings account

If you are not old enough to open a bank account yet, then your parents' banking institutions may provide a teen or student savings account which you can utilize. One great way to start saving is by using a savings account to set aside money for your birthday, graduation, or future emergencies.

Using a savings account is a great way to save money, instead of stashing your checks or cash away in a drawer. In addition, a savings account can help you to get interest on your deposits, which can increase your savings over time.

In addition, you can automate your pay checks by directly depositing your pay check into two different accounts, the checking account and the savings account. When you automate your pay check, a portion of the money will directly go to a savings account before you can use it.

Set financial goals for yourself

You should set clear financial goals. For instance, you should know what you are saving up for, whether it is for college, buying your first car or even a new phone. When you know exactly what you are saving money for, you will know the amount of money you need to save.

After that, you can break down your big savings goals into smaller and more achievable ones. For example, if you want to save $1,500 for a deposit on your first car, you can set a goal of putting aside $50 every week. This will enable you to save for your car in 20 weeks.

Create a budget

Create a budget and stick to it. Calculate the money you earn every month through your jobs or allowance. Then, calculate the total amount of money that you need to use every month for your needs and wants, and deduct that from your income. Put aside the remaining money in your account.

After that, you can use your budget to monitor the amount of money you are earning, how much money you are spending and what expenses you can sacrifice in order to reach your saving goals quicker.

Take advantage of discounts

If you want to occasionally make big purchases while still saving for other goals, then you should take advantage of discounts and sales. For instance, many expensive products like computers and phones go on sale sometimes, and if you buy them during that period, you will spend less money and remain with some cash to put towards your saving goals.

You should track the price of the product that you are planning to buy and if the price comes down, then you may consider buying it. Although this takes patience, it will help you to stick to your savings plan.

You can buy refurbished or second-hand products

There are many second-hand products that are being sold cheaply compared to brand new ones. You can opt to buy second-hand goods online or in thrift stores if you want to save a substantial amount of money in the long run.

Involve your parents in your saving plan

A good way to stay motivated throughout your saving journey is to involve your parents. They can keep you accountable and even offer financial support along the way.

For example, if you are planning to save $3,000 for a car, your parents may match that amount with $3,000 s you can afford to buy a car worth $6,000. That would be easier than raising $6,000 on your won.

Use cash instead of cards

Credit cards are good because they can help you build credit, while debit cards allow you to access the money that has been deposited into your checking account. However, although these cards are good, if you struggle with impulse buying or overspending, then you should occasionally leave your cards at home and use cash instead.

Studies indicate that someone who uses cash instead of cards will actually spend less money because they are fully aware about the prices of the products they are buying and the limitations. However, when they use a credit or debit card, they feel like they have unlimited money, which leads to overspending and impulse buying.

Therefore, if you want to go shopping with your friends at the mall, you should only put the exact amount of cash that you want to spend in your wallet.

Teenagers need to know how to manage their money as they get closer to adulthood. Attaining financial literacy as a teen can help you to become self-reliant, become financially disciplined and even gain confidence. In addition, it can help you get started on the journey to financial freedom, financial independence and financial security.

11

YOUNG ADULT: THE COLLEGE STUDENT SURVIVAL GUIDE (HOW TO KEEP YOUR FINANCIAL STABILITY THROUGHOUT COLLEGE)

Unfortunately, 42 million Americans have student loan debts. The debt is not only owed by current students and recent graduates, it also includes people who completed their studies decades ago. Currently, the total student loan debt owed by the borrowers amounts to $1.75 trillion.

Some undergraduate and graduate students decide to borrow student loans because it is necessary for them to complete their studies. However, others unfortunately borrow these loans because they are not well informed.

College or university tuition fees are high and you may think it may be easier to just borrow the student loan debt now and pay it later after graduating. The reality is, although student loans may help you finish university, they can be overwhelming to pay off and may cause a lot of stress. The good news is, you can learn how to pay for your college fees and complete your studies without accumulating any student loan debts.

However, we will first look at experiences of people who borrowed their student loans and how it affected them later on in life.

John Brown is 62 years old and has a student loan debt amounting to $299,081. Brown currently works part time in a dental office as a book keeper and a trainer with the National conflict resolution centre. He earns a salary which is less than $2,000 per month.

Brown borrowed the student loan for medical school and he had planned to pay it off after completing the medical training. Unfortunately, he did not manage to finish his postgraduate training in the United States and he does not have a medical license to practice as a physician.

Brown says he will never be able to repay the outstanding loan balance of $299, 081, which keeps growing because of the accrued interest rate. Although Brown's only way to repay this loan is to keep working, the 62-year-old is not able to work fulltime because of his health challenges.

Jane Shonda, who is 65 years old, has been teaching since 2008, but is now struggling to get a full-time teaching job because of her advanced age. Shonda has a student loan debt of $100,000, which she accrued by studying for her master's degree in order to become a qualified teacher.

Shonda has applied to over 300 jobs within a period of 3 years but she keeps getting turned down. Even though Shonda would love to start teaching full-time again, she cannot because school districts will only hire her as a substitute teacher.

Shonda said she will never be able to pay off the $100,000 student loan debt unless she stops buying groceries, utilities and gas in her home. The loan debt repayment situation has caused her to develop depression and she has been put on depression medication by her doctor.

Hailey Orona attended Brooks Institute of Photography from 2005 to 2007 and has a student loan debt of more than $200,000. Most of the student loan debts are private. Orona has been repaying the loans for the past seven years and her parents have been helping her pay the loans but in smaller amounts. According to Orona, her debts have not gone down because of the high interest rates.

In addition, she does not qualify for the debt relief since she has been repaying the loans. Orona admitted that she has only been repaying the loan because her parents were co-signers of the loans and they will get affected if she starts defaulting on the loan repayment.

From the stories above, you can see that getting student loan debts is not the best way to pay for college or university education, because not only does repaying the loan take years, but it may also affect your physical, emotional, mental and financial wellbeing.

If you have made up your mind that you do not want to borrow any student loans, then you can follow the tips below to become financially stable and finish your education without accruing any debts.

TIPS TO USE BEFORE YOU BEGIN YOUR DEGREE

1. Start working now

The best way to avoid debts is to earn an income and pay for your education yourself. It is understandable that this option may not always be possible and with the high tuition fees, it may be difficult to raise the full tuition.

However, you need to understand that paying for a portion of your tuition with your income will make a huge impact. If you start earning money as soon as possible and save for your university degree, you will not depend on banks and will not need to borrow any loans.

1. Excel in your studies

Another great way of avoiding student debts is to excel in your studies in high school. If you excel in your courses in high school, you can qualify for scholarships and grants. These scholarships and grants can sometimes fund your full tuition. The great thing about scholarships and grants is, you do not need to pay that money back.

1. Apply for grants and scholarships

If you have been wondering where you can apply for these scholarships and grants, then you will be pleased to know that every university or college has its own grants and scholarships that students can apply for. Moreover, there are needs-based and merit-based scholarships.

Therefore, if you want to attend a particular university or college, just check out their website to find out what grants or scholarships they offer their students. If all the scholarships and grants are relevant to your situation, then you can apply to all of them.

In addition, not every scholarship has to be from the school that you want to attend because there are some external programs that are offered to students.

1. **Select an affordable university or college**

The cost of university and college education is rising globally. However, there are affordable learning institutions that are available. For instance, a public, four-year, in-state college will have less tuition compared to a prestigious university.

In addition, there are countries that offer free university education, like France and Germany.

1. **Speed up your time in university or college**

You can speed up your time in college and avoid debts by utilising programs like AP and CLEP tests. You can do Advanced Placement (AP) courses while you are in high school by signing up for the classes in your school. If you pass the test, it will transfer for college credit and you will not have to pay for them later on.

Testing programs like the CLEP test allows you to test out courses and get college credits for them. This will help you to avoid paying to learn subjects that you have already mastered.

TIPS TO USE IF YOU ARE ALREADY STUDYING

1. Discuss the tuition with your parents

If your parents will help to pay for university, then you should converse with them about saving for your tuition beforehand, which will help you to avoid student debts. You can also talk to them about savings options that offer additional benefits for college savings, such as a 529b.

You should have this discussion with your parents as early as possible. This conversation will also help you to know how much tuition your parents will pay and how much money you will need to raise on your own.

1. Work part-time while you are studying

If you are studying part-time, then you can also work part-time to fund your college education. However, many students usually study full-time with the aim of finishing their studies sooner to start working.

Therefore, if you study full-time, then you can work full-time during the summers and during evenings. In addition, you can do remote jobs from home or look for freelancing gigs which can help you to earn extra money without being overwhelming. You can look for these freelancing jobs on online platforms like Fivver and Upwork.

1. **Work on-campus**

A great way to reduce your college tuition is to find work on campus. For example, if you are a Resident Advisor or a student leader in your university or college dorm, then you may get benefits like discounts on food or housing while at campus.

This will lower the expenses significantly, and you can put the money you save from these discounts towards your tuition expenses. If you think this is a great option for you, then you can enrol for work-study programs which will give you the option of working on-campus for reduced tuition expenses.

Additionally, you can choose a low-maintenance job like working in an administrative environment or in a library can enable you to complete your assignments when you are not helping other students.

1. **Follow an effective budget**

You should make choices that are cost-effective in order to save more money. For example, you can buy second-hand text books or look for free ones instead of buying new ones. In addition, you can live with roommates on-campus or close to the university to reduce your rental costs.

Furthermore, you can buy and cook your food in your room as much as you can. This will help you to reduce the number of times you eat out, and the amount of money you will spend doing so.

Moreover, avoid opening up credit cards because they may seem appealing at first, but the debts will add up and you don't need to start dealing with debt repayment when you graduate and start your life.

1. **Consider doing hybrid learning**

The rise in popularity of online education has created unique opportunities for students in this day and age. For example, students can choose to enrol in hybrid education, which is the merging of online education with on-campus classes.

Hybrid education is more affordable than in-person learning and it still offers the occasional on-campus experience which enables the student to experience wholistic education. For instance, a hybrid program can help you to avoid costs which are not associated with learning, like transportation expenses and childcare.

In addition, hybrid programs will give you greater flexibility because you will have the option to complete the coursework at your own schedule. This will enable you to get more hours to work and earn more income for your college or university tuition.

1. **Research about repayment plans**

You should talk to your university or college about their repayment plan options. For instance, instead of paying for your tuition upfront, you can enter into a repayment plan which can spread out your tuition expenses over a long period of time. This is a much better option than student loan debts, because it is interest-free.

1. **Crowdfunding**

You can ask your family members, your friends and any other people around you to help you fund your education. Although crowdfunding is a relatively new thing, it may slowly gain popularity because students are becoming more creative in their process of trying to study without accruing any debts.

1. **Employer Tuition Reimbursement**

Some companies are willing to pay part or full tuition for their employees. This is beneficial to the employers because it builds longevity and loyalty in the company and it also benefits the employee because they won't have to pay for their tuition.

However, these company programs depend on variables like eligible programs, your grades and the cost of the program. Therefore, if you do not have a job, you should consider applying to the companies that offer tuition reimbursement. Examples of companies that offer this opportunity include Wells Fargo, Starbucks, Verizon and UPS.

In conclusion, university and college fees can be very costly and the student loan industry has become very massive. This is why you should explore options that will help you to avoid student loan debt.

Hopefully, these tips can help you to complete your studies without the burden of having thousands of dollars in student loan debts, so you can graduate debt-free and start living life to the fullest.

CONCLUSION

This book contains a lot of important financial strategies and if you follow them, you can build wealth and kickstart your journey to becoming financially independent. The book contains important lessons like;

1. ELIMINATING DEBT STRATEGIES

We all know that being in debt is a very terrible feeling because it looms over you like a dark cloud, preventing you from living your best life and hindering your financial goals, like buying a house, saving for retirement or even going on your dream vacation.

If you have a huge debt totalling thousands of dollars or hundreds of thousands of dollars, you need to know that your debt does not need to last forever. You can pay it all off in time if you stick to a plan and follow some financial tips outlined here. If you are tired of owing thousands of dollars in debt, then

CONCLUSION

getting out of debt should be your number one priority for your cash.

1. **SAVING AND BUDGETING**

A budget is a plan on how you will spend the money you earn and it helps you live within your means, cut costs and grow your wealth. When you create and follow a budget, you will always have enough money to make it through the month, even if you have a low income.

One surprising thing about budgeting and saving your money is, you will feel like you got a salary increase because you will know where your money is going and you can use more of it appropriately. Both budgeting and saving are very important actions that go hand in hand if you want to build wealth.

1. **INVESTING**

Investing is the act of buying financial assets like bonds and stocks, with the expectation that those assets will increase in value overtime and earn you profits in the long run. There are many different types of investments that are accessible to every person, regardless of your age, career or income and they have been covered in this chapter.

Black women can increase their wealth by purchasing assets at very low prices and selling them at higher prices in future. Investing is a great way to enable your money to outpace inflation and increase in value over a long period.

1. **SIDE HUSTLE OPTIONS**

CONCLUSION

If you already have a job to cater to your basic needs but you need more money to supplement your income, you can start a side hustle. There are many remote side hustles which give you the opportunity to work from home, so if you already have a 9-5 job, you can do the side hustle during your off days, after work or even during holidays and earn extra money to make your life more comfortable.

Moreover, there are some side hustles that allow you to earn passive income, therefore, once you start them, all you have to do is relax and let the money come in. Side hustles can be a game changer that can make a big impact in your purse, and if you do it right, you can successfully turn your part-time job into one of your main sources of income.

1. EMERGENCY FUND – HOW IT WORKS AND HOW TO SET IT UP

An emergency fund is money that you set aside so you can use it when you are in financial distress. The main aim of building an emergency fund is to improve your financial security by creating a pool of funds that you can use to meet unexpected and sudden expenses. When you have an emergency fund, you will not need to borrow high-interest debt options like unsecured loans or shylocks when you are experiencing a financial crisis.

You should follow the tips outlined in this book to open an emergency fund for the following reasons;

1. **To avoid accruing more debts**

An emergency fund can help you to stop adding to your debts whenever you encounter any financial challenges. It can help

CONCLUSION

you to cover things you have not budgeted for, such as medical expenses and vehicle repairs. You can use the emergency funds to handle financially stressful emergencies, which will in turn help you to stay focused on your path towards becoming debt free.

1. **If are new at budgeting**

When you begin budgeting, you can mistakenly leave out some very important expenses that you need to plan for. In such instances, the fund can help you to cover those expenses during the first year, and then you can add them into your budget in future.

1. **If you only have one stream of income**

If you only have one job, then you should have a substantial emergency fund. The fund can help you and your family to get out of emergencies like illnesses that prevent the breadwinner from working or unexpected job losses. When you have money that can cover your expenses for at least 6 months, then it can cushion you and your family if the unexpected happens.

1. **If you are self-employed**

If you are self-employed, if you are on a job contract or if you are an independent contractor, then you need to put sufficient funds in place. In addition, if you see that the contract is coming to an end, you should work hard and save up more in your emergency fund.

CONCLUSION

1. **RETIREMENT PLAN**

Retirement planning is what you do to prepare yourself for life after you stop working when you attain the retirement age. It involves setting aside enough money to cover all your expenses when you stop working during retirement. Every woman should strive to put aside enough funds to support them when they retire in old age and they can do so using the strategies talked about in this chapter.

1. **STARTING YOUR OWN BUSINESS**

Starting a business is a very interesting, rewarding and fun experience. Unfortunately, many black women want to start a business but they don't know where to begin. The good news is, this book has shared tips that can help you to successfully start your business.

1. **TEENAGE DIARIES: TIPS ON HOW TO MAKE AN ENTRANCE IN THE BUSINESS WORLD (BEST SAVING STRATEGIES AND SO ON)**

Saving cash is simple. It just involves spending less than you earn every month and putting the extra money somewhere safe. Teenagers need to know how to manage their money as they get closer to adulthood.

Attaining financial literacy as a teen can help you to become self-reliant, become financially disciplined and even gain confidence. In addition, it can help you get started on the journey to financial freedom, financial independence and financial security.

1. **YOUNG ADULT: THE COLLEGE STUDENT SURVIVAL GUIDE (HOW TO KEEP YOUR FINANCIAL STABILITY THROUGHOUT COLLEGE WITHOUT INDEBTING)**

Some undergraduate and graduate students decide to borrow student loans because it is necessary for them to complete their studies. However, others unfortunately borrow these loans because they are not well informed.

The reality is, although student loans may help you finish university, they can be overwhelming to pay off and may cause a lot of stress. This chapter highlights how you can pay for your college fees and complete your studies without accumulating any student loan debts.

ATTAINING FINANCIAL FREEDOM

If you implement the financial literacy lessons outlined in this book, you will eventually attain financial independence and financial freedom. As a result, you will reap the following benefits after attaining financial freedom;

1. **You will have more disposable income**

After paying for your needs and recurrent expenses every month, you will have more extra money to spend on whatever you want. This means you will be able to use your money on things that make you happy and on activities that you enjoy, rather than on necessities only.

1. **It will improve your mental health**

If you are always worried about money, it can negatively affect your emotional wellbeing. However, when you are financially independent and free, you will be able to relax and enjoy your life.

1. **Your lifestyle will improve**

Since you will have more disposable income, you will be able to afford higher-quality services and goods, including nicer clothes, vacations and a nicer home.

1. **Your relationships will improve**

When you attain financial freedom, your relationships may also improve. Since you are not worried or stressed about cash, you can focus on your relationships more and make them stronger.

In addition, if you have a spouse, it will improve your relationship because you will feel less overall stress, you will have more quality time together and you may be closer to him or her.

1. **You will get more free time**

If you aren't worried about money, you will have the time to focus on other things that are important to you, like spending more time with family and friends, taking some time off to relax, or pursue your hobbies and dreams.

CONCLUSION

1. **You will have access to more opportunities**

When you achieve financial freedom, you will have more opportunities and you will also have the ability to take advantage of those opportunities without worrying about how it can affect your finances.

1. **It will boost your confidence**

Financial freedom may make you become more confident. It can help you become more confident in your health, looks, relationships, communication, careers and life choices.

1. **You will have less stress**

Financial freedom will lessen your stress because you will not have to worry about having inadequate cash to cater to your expenses. In addition, it will give you more peace of mind and you will feel more at ease.

1. **You will have greater financial independence**

If you are financially free, you will have more financial independence. This means you will not depend on other people for financial support. Therefore, you will be in a position to make your own financial decisions and control your future.

ATTAINING FINANCIAL FINANCIALLY INDEPENDENCE

CONCLUSION

There are some women who believe that it is better to fully depend on other people financially. Although this sounds like an easy option, every woman should also strive to attain financial independence.

This book has provided strategies on how black women can become financially independent and if you implement them, you can enjoy the following benefits of being a financially independent woman;

- **You become self-sufficient and self-reliant**

Financial independence enables you to pay for most of your basic needs and wants. However, when you depend on someone else, you will have to wait for them to take care of your needs, which can be very frustrating, especially if those people have financial problems or are unreliable. Being self-reliant does not mean that you should never ask for help. It means that you can pay for all your immediate needs and wants using your income.

- **You are free to make your own choices and decisions**

Some women who financially depend on their spouses or partners do not have the authority or power to make major decisions in their marriages or relationships. In fact, you may find yourself in a situation where your partner controls and dictates your life if they are the sole breadwinner in the marriage. This can make it difficult for you to share your opinions or make choices because you don't have your own money or the power to do so.

- **It prevents abuse**

CONCLUSION

Unfortunately, some women who are in abusive relationships don't want to leave because they financially depend on their partners. If you are financially stable, you can leave an abusive marriage or relationship and support yourself financially. That is why you should prioritise your career and education so that you don't endure abuse because of lack of finances to leave the home permanently.

- **It increases your sense of self-worth**

Although money is not everything, earning an income and spending it however you want will influence how you feel as a person. Women who are financially independent tend to feel more confident about themselves and usually have a higher self-esteem.

- **To keep up with inflation**

Inflation has been slowly increasing over the years and now, the cost of owning a good home, enrolling your children in quality schools and maintaining a comfortable standard of living is expensive. Therefore, a household with two incomes is better. If a woman is earning her own money, she can pay some of the household expenses and also contribute to the family's long-term financial objectives.

ATTAINING FINANCIAL LITERACY

This book has strategies that you can use to become financially literate. When you become financially literate, you will become empowered to make smarter decisions when it comes to your income. In addition, financial literacy will drastically improve your life in the following ways;

- **It will prepare you for any emergencies**

Financial literacy skills like saving prepares you for any unforeseen emergencies. For example, getting laid off or getting a salary decrease can negatively affect you. However, you can cushion yourself from such problems by putting money into their savings and emergency savings accounts.

- **It will help you reach your goals**

When you fully understand how to budget and save your money, you can create plans that will hold you accountable to your finances and help you achieve financial goals that seem unachievable. For example, although you may not be able to afford something that you would like to do, like travelling abroad, you can create a plan to increase your chances of making it happen.

- **It will help you achieve financial confidence**

When you have knowledge about finances, you can make major life choices confidently knowing that you are less likely to be affected by unforeseen negative outcomes.

- **It will help you avoid making devastating mistakes**

CONCLUSION

Some innocent financial decisions can have very serious and long-term implications that can cost you money or negatively affect your life plans. However, financial literacy can help you avoid making any mistakes with your personal finance.

To conclude, all black women can become financially literate and financially disciplined. Financial discipline will help all black women to establish control over their finances and use their money as a tool to freely make choices that help them feel more satisfied in life. Moreover, it will enable them to build generational wealth while enjoying their lives to the fullest.

Printed in Poland
by Amazon Fulfillment
Poland Sp. z o.o., Wrocław